CONTENTS

Key to Kitchen plans

C	Cooker
D	Dryer
DW	Dishwasher
FS	Food storage
G	General storage
H	Cooking hob
HP	Hot plate
G/EO	Gas/Electric oven
R	Refrigerator
S	Sink unit
T	Table
W	Window
WM	Washing machine
WT	Work top
SH	Shelves
SC	Suspended ceiling
WD	Waste-disposer
U	Units
DW	Dishwasher

D1517406

Metric note: 1 inch = 2.54 centimetres
                 1 foot = 30.48 centimetres
                 6 feet = 1.83 metres

About this book

Whatever your taste, whatever your available space, you will find lots of ideas to tantalise and tempt you among these fifty fabulous designs that range from the simple to the sumptuous, from dream kitchens to attic kitchens and a kitchen in a cupboard, from open family rooms to striking colour schemes and cosy sitting areas for two.

Are you re-planning your home or planning a new one? Have you been hunting frantically for schemes that are clear and refreshing or do you want rooms that are warm and comfortable? Are you exasperated with inspired ideas that frankly aren't practical? Or is it glamour and flair that you are after?

Take your choice. Adopt an entire design or take just one idea from any or all of these exciting pages and adapt it to your own very special requirements.

Versatility is the keyword to the designs in the Golden Homes Book of Kitchens and Living Rooms. And we've chosen the two most important rooms in your house with which to start this new series of books that will offer you ideas for every corner and facet of your home.

Maybe our ideas will prompt ideas of your own.

Kitchens and Living rooms

A Golden Hands book

Marshall Cavendish, London

Published by Marshall Cavendish Publications Ltd,
58 Old Compton Street, London WIV 5PA
© *Marshall Cavendish Ltd, 1972,*
58 Old Compton Street, London WIV 5PA
This material first published by Marshall Cavendish Ltd in:
Kitchens: 25 New Designs
Living Rooms: 25 New Designs
This volume first published 1973
Printed by: Text—Petty & Sons, Leeds
       Prelims—Brenard Press, Hounslow
       Bound by—Acfords, Chichester
ISBN 0 85685 020 9
This volume is not to be sold in the U.S.A., Canada and the Philippines

KITCHENS
The First Principles

1 Kitchens should be tailored as far as possible to the particular needs of the family. Husband and wife both out at work all day? Then labour-saving is a priority. Is it a large family? This dictates the desirable size of the kitchen, specially the size of the 'living' area. Are there children? If they are toddlers, the housewife in the kitchen has to keep an eye on them; yet they must be protected from hot pans and other hazards. One solution: a see-through divider between working area and play/living area. Are shops near or distant – requiring modest or substantial storage? Does the family do much entertaining? If so, appliances – from electric mixers to dishwashers – should be geared to hospitality.

2 The shape of the room dictates the kitchen arrangement. A long, narrow room lends itself to a galley; a rectangle to an L-shape; a square to a U-shape.

3 Easy access to the kitchen is vital: perhaps a hatch, rather than a space-wasting door, to the living room if most meals are served there.

4 Good lighting, natural and artificial, is vital too. Enlarge a window? Replace small panes with a single sheet of glass? Certainly spotlight work areas.

5 Also vital: adequate ventilation. Cooking smells can permeate the whole house. The answer: an extractor fan and/or a hood above the cooker.

6 Place the sink and the cooker in line or at right-angles, linked ideally by a spacious working surface. The fridge and storage cupboards can then be grouped in the order that best suits the shape of the room and the house-wife's needs.

7 Maximum storage and work surfaces – but minimum floor space. If that principle is not observed in the functional part of the kitchen, the housewife will to and fro many unnecessary miles during the year. Equally, there must be a place for everything and everything should be in its place. Ideally, the utensils and containers the cook uses most should be almost within arm's length when she is preparing meals. And the storage of utensils and crockery should be arranged so that they can be easily mobilised and replaced in position without re-arranging less essential things, let alone perching on a stool.

8 Easily washable floor, walls and ceiling, the avoidance of dust and grime traps are priorities in planning. Castor-based heavy appliances enable you to pull them out and clean behind them.

9 Every kitchen, however small, should have somewhere where a meal can be eaten – if only a pull-out flap and a stool.

10 But there is a big difference between a kitchen where the dining part is the only dining area in the house and a kitchen used just occasionally for informal family meals. In the first case, the kitchen must be planned so that food preparation can be hidden from view during the actual meal. In the second case, make sure that the dining end of the kitchen is comfortable and easy to clear up and clean.

KITCHEN THAT'S A BACHELOR'S DELIGHT

It contains all the
basic equipment slotted
tidily into a small area.
And every inch of wall space
is used for storage

It's a tiny miracle! Only 37½ sq. ft. (3.5 sq. m.), it has everything the cook needs, yet looks neither cramped nor untidy.

The largest item is the fridge — built-in at eye level to the right of the picture — with a deep-freezing compartment and lots of storage space to compensate for the lack of a larder in this kitchen. There is room for a 'baby' cooker to sit next to the stainless steel sink; a power point at the other end of the 'L' shape takes the pressure cooker and the electric kettle.

Every inch of wall space has been used for storage cupboards, set both above and below the continuous working surface that runs from the fridge to below the window. The short wall facing the 'L' has been used to advantage by fixing a wood batten to hold hooks for tea towels, pot holders, the odd extra pan and the kitchen chair, which folds up and hangs when not in use.

The 'table' is a flap that pulls out underneath the window, giving enough elbow room for one person to enjoy eating with a view. Even when it is raining, the yellow and white decor makes this a light and airy corner, full of charm. The roller blind echoes the colour scheme and cunning use of wide, horizontal stripes makes the window seem even wider than it is.

Ideas worth adopting. Where space is at a premium, putting up a wooden rail on the wall and painting it to match is the sort of inexpensive job that any handyman or woman can tackle. It costs little, and gives valuable hanging space.

Painting the front of the fridge (or other bulky items) to match the decor, as in this kitchen, has the welcome effect of making it blend into the rest of the room.

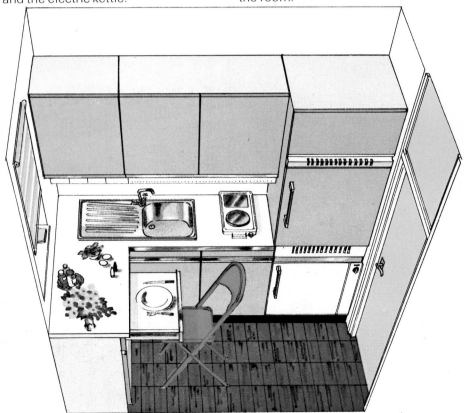

This drawing shows the kitchen from another angle, with an average-size oven fitted in under the fridge. Alternatively, a small washing machine on castors could go under the fridge

Camera Press

KITCHEN WITH A COUNTRY FLAVOUR

2 Old beams and mellow tiles; the original stable door; a view of the garden . . . it's a capacious kitchen/dining area that combines tradition with efficiency

Here is a beautiful kitchen/cum/dining room where old mixes happily with new. Clever design has cut the kitchen area back to a compact section, separated from the more roomy dining end by a peninsular unit.

The oven area follows a sensible work sequence, starting from the end wall of the room, where the oven has been mounted at eye level. Running back from this to the sink is a continuous work top for food preparation. Next comes the peninsular unit which holds the cooking hobs; these can double as a hot plate for serving food to the dining area. This peninsular unit has storage cupboards on both sides to service the kitchen and dining area respectively. And there's plenty more storage space in the streamlined modern cupboards built in both above and below the work surfaces.

The kitchen has strip lighting set flush under the wall cupboards. This is supplemented by crafty spotlights set among the beams. In the dining area, the original stable door has a glass panel set into it to give extra daylight, and a view of the garden. The ceramic tiles on the floor are easy to

John Prizeman

mop and echo the traditional feel of the beams.

The dining area is essentially a family room, and the round dining table will take more chairs than a square or oblong counterpart would.

Ideas worth adopting. Staining and lacquering both the door and beams the same colour — blue in this case — links the dining and kitchen areas. The blue contrasts with the functional white of the units, appliances and ceiling. An archway, here housing the fridge with wine storage above the fridge, makes a graceful alternative to a square cupboard.

**Opposite page: view of dining area
Above: view through to
end wall of kitchen area
Left: floor plan of
both areas**

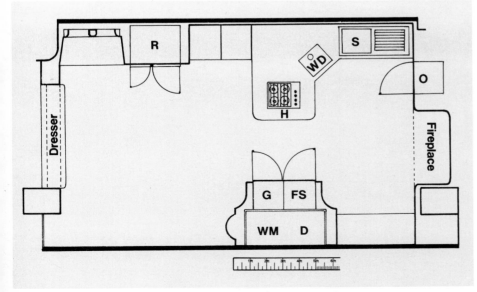

Here is a modern family
kitchen, so well laid out
that entertaining
on a grand scale
need cause no more flurry
than an everyday meal

This beautiful kitchen is interesting because it uses a standard range of kitchen fitments with the addition of custom-made in-fill units for maximum flexibility.

The overall shape is rectangular. A large central island unit houses the cooker hobs, offers plenty of storage space conveniently and reduces the floor area. Opposite the island unit — and making the most of the view through what is virtually a window wall — is a triple sink with a waste-disposer in the central bowl. Under the work top, just visible in the foreground of the picture, is a double oven and the dishwasher. Glass-fronted cupboards provide a link with the dining area. The drawers in this fitment, which are designed to match the rest of the kitchen units, are placed near the dishwasher, so that cutlery from the dishwasher can be stored on the spot.

A custom-built hood over the island unit hobs takes care of cooking smells at the source, and two of the windows are fitted with adjustable glass louvres. Artificial light is housed in the suspended, tiled ceiling and consists of set-in spotlights and a long fluorescent strip over the sink. An angled spotlight over the island unit provides the cook with extra brightness.

Ideas worth adopting: the island fitment, which could be added to a U-shaped kitchen; and the lighting arrangements set into the suspended ceiling, including the long strip light over the sink.

Floor plan of the kitchen area

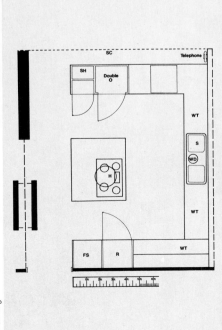

KITCHEN THAT'S COMPLETE ON A WALL 4

Just twelve feet
(3.65 metres) long,
it contains everything
the housewife needs
for cooking and leaves
the rest of the room free
for dining and relaxing

What better solution for the one-room flat than the one-wall kitchen? This neat and pretty one was designed to fulfil one of the ideals of kitchen planning – the siting of cooker and sink on the same stretch of work surface, with a distance of about 3 ft. 6 in. (1.06 mm.) between the two.

Hygiene is high on the list of priorities for one-room living and the designer has made this easy by covering the entire work top and the wall behind it as well as the base of the units with heat-proof white ceramic tiles. The result is a cool and efficient bank of custom-made units incorporating a built-in cooker (with an extractor hood over it), a double sink with a waste-disposer, a built-in fridge and a dishwasher fitted in near the sink.

The open shelves across the top of the kitchen lend an informal note with their brightly coloured casserole dishes, and a narrow shelf between wall and floor cupboards is the perfect place for glass storage jars.

The dining end is warm and inviting, with the floor sanded to a glowing colour and sealed to protect it from kitchen stains. A sturdy pine table and graceful Bentwood chairs with warm orange cushions are a good foil to the white of the kitchen units.

Although the kitchen units have been custom-made, a handyman could copy the impeccable layout by using whitewood fitments.

Below: plan and elevation of the kitchen

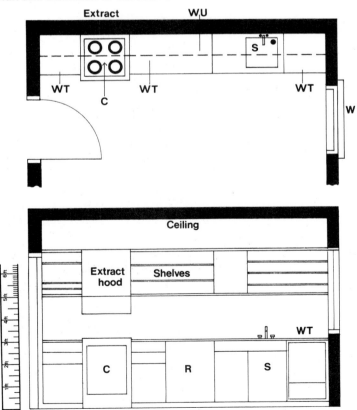

THIS KITCHEN
IS MADE TO
MEASURE   5

THIS KITCHEN IS MADE TO MEASURE 5

It had to be, to suit this new concept in kitchen design — a wedge shape created by dividing the open-plan living room diagonally

Application of a lively imagination to kitchen design is reflected in this warm and attractive kitchen — in the shaping of it, in the use of old and new materials and in the unusual design of the units.

Virtually wedge-shaped, the working area is divided from the living area by the beautiful specially designed fitment in the background of the picture on the previous page. Like a long arm, it juts diagonally across the area and it incorporates the sink unit and the hot plates, culminating in the fitment at the far right, which houses the oven built-in over the fridge.

The cupboards in the fitment are framed in warm iroko wood with black tops and door panels. Black laminated plastic is used to face the doors and to cover the work tops.

Part of the structural conversion in the basement of the house consisted of the introduction of cavity walls at intervals to counteract damp. The architect used these to house the central heating and other pipes. The unusually shaped cupboard on the left of the photograph backs on to one of these walls. Painted white, it blends in with the wall when closed. It provides quite a lot of storage space and the top cupboard door lets down to act as an extra work top.

The colour scheme is one of the charms of this kitchen. The colours of the quarry tiles blend beautifully with the warm colour of the wood and the smart black of the cupboards. The rest of the room is white, with the exception of the lowered wooden ceiling which is painted sage green.

Ideas worth adopting. Note the space-saving and attractive use of glass shelves on a steel frame, used in the alcove at the centre of the picture. Lit by spotlights hidden in the ceiling and filled with glass storage jars, this helps to provide extra storage in a small kitchen as well as being a decorative feature. The dining end of the kitchen is furnished with a pine table and unassuming kitchen chairs; yet they blend in perfectly with the more sophisticated kitchen area. The divider unit makes a good job of cutting off the kitchen from the living room, yet allows light from the living room window to reach the kitchen.

Don Kidman

Illustration shows the entire kitchen/living area; close-up of the kitchen is shown on the previous page

KITCHEN BUILT INTO A BAY

6

Suspended on the first floor of a small house, it takes up no ground space. A skylight in place of windows saves wall space and ensures privacy

This tiny, all-wood kitchen measures only about 4 ft. (1.2 metres) by 8 ft. 6 in. (2.6 metres).

It's housed in a bay built on to a small house. As the bay overlooks the garden of the main house, it was built with no windows to ensure privacy in the garden. But the large skylight more than compensates for the lack of windows.

Wood is the unifying material. It has been used to cover the walls and the kitchen units, all custom-built by a local cabinet maker, in Canadian Douglas fir. Teak makes a practical surface for all the work tops.

The space-saving layout includes a small electric cooker built in over a small fridge. The sink is beyond the work top on right of picture.

The dining table is white laminated plastic, edged with natural wood to echo the wood in the rest of the room. Vinyl tiles are used on the floor in the area close to the kitchen, but the rest of the room is carpeted with the same inexpensive carpet used throughout the whole small house to avoid too many colours in a small area.

Extra storage space is provided by three narrow shelves under the skylight, and well-placed spotlights give light over the work surfaces.

It is interesting to see how the use of wood makes this small kitchen blend into the rest of the room unobtrusively.

Brecht Einzig

13

KITCHEN THAT WAS ADDED

Elizabeth Whiting

Clever design is
the essence of this
ultra-modern kitchen
addition to an old house,
linked with the garden
by its unusual
angled wall of windows

**Left: custom-built cooker unit
houses the oven, and has
a streamlined arm holding
the extractor hood over the hobs
Above: louvres set in
the windows give
adequate ventilation;
spotlights on a track
give extra light
in the cooking area at night**

This ingenious and unusual kitchen is fitted with the best of today's equipment, but also makes use of traditional materials like wood and quarry tiles which are in sympathy with the old part of the house, although no attempt has been made to blend the old and the new.

Everything about this kitchen is exciting. There is the unusually angled wall of windows, with its view of sky and trees and the neighbouring old houses. By contrast within the kitchen itself, there is the streamlined shape of the cooker hood — echoed in the fitment which houses the fridge and freezer.

The warm wooden ceiling is fitted with spotlights and a track of adjustable spotlights hangs at the top of

the windows, making this kitchen as bright by night as it is by day.

The kitchen is basically a galley type with a double sink and waste disposer at one end, and the fridge and freezer built into one unit at the other end. The long fitment on the window wall incorporates the split level cooker (the cooker hood is designed as a streamlined arm of the unit which houses the waist-level oven) and a small extra sink.

All the units in this kitchen are custom-made and include useful extras like a marble pastry board (supremely cold for kneading dough), let into one of the worktops, and a wooden chopping board which can be lifted out of one of the units.

A teak room divider, running

Don Kidman

parallel with the window wall, cuts off the kitchen area from the living room. Ventilation is provided by adjustable glass louvres set at intervals in the wall of glass; a long ledge running along in front of the windows makes very useful standing room for a vast array of glass jars containing items in everyday use.

This is a marvellous cook's kitchen, styled for efficiency but with a strong bias towards good looks. All the materials used in it are beautiful — the teak worktops, the warm quarry-tiled floor, the handsome wooden ceiling,

and the vast quantity of glass which allows the sun to pour in from all sides.

Ideas worth adopting: the impeccable layout, with the sink at one end, the fridge and freezer at the other, and the hob and oven in the centre with plenty of worktops and storage space in between; the track of adjustable spotlights, hung on the ceiling, which allows flexibility of lighting; the combination of very modern equipment with traditional materials like wood and quarry tiles, which results in a kitchen full of exciting contrasts.

This illustration shows how the kitchen pictured here and on previous page is linked to the open-plan living room by a set of three tiled steps; note the wall of windows which matches the glass wall at the kitchen end

This is the ideal solution for anyone living in a small room, where space is at a premium, and this kind of unit can be constructed cheaply to fit into the space available.

Doors fitted in front of the sink and storage area turn the fitting into a cupboard, and shut off the unit completely when not in use. A section of wall jutting out level with the line of the open cupboard doors hides the unit from view from the living end of the room.

At eye-level, slim-line shelves have been made deliberately shallow to allow hanging room for tea towels on a plastic rack screwed to the inside of the doors; these shelves take sufficient crockery and linen to cater for one or two people.

A single sink is fitted in the corner on the right, leaving sufficient space at the back of it to stand a plastic plate drainer. The stainless steel square holds the electric cooking hobs. Below, on one side is the fridge; the other side houses a fitted cupboard for food storage and pots and pans.

Ventilation is important in a confined cooking space; here holes cut into the back of the fitment above the hobs connect to a ventilation shelf in the wall behind.

Ideas worth adopting. Still using the same area of space inside this compact unit, the choice of equipment could be varied to suit individual requirements. For example, a slightly smaller fridge could be fitted on the right under the sink, leaving room to put a small oven under the burners, over a small storage cupboard, on the left-hand side.

KITCHEN THAT GOES INTO A CUPBOARD

Simple enough for a handyman to build at home; perfect for a bed-sitting room, since it uses little space and can be shut off completely

Michael Boys

The old brick floor,
family size cooking range
and pine furniture combine
with a modern working plan
that brings this
17th century room up to date

This delightful kitchen with a farmhouse atmosphere is in fact in a town house. Its casual rustic look veils a well-thought-out working plan. The large fridge in the corner is next to a useful work top which leads logically to the capacious and versatile cooking range. This particular model is oil-fired, which does away with cleaning and riddling and provides plenty of hot water as well as an ever-warm and welcoming kitchen. The work top next to the range has a marble slab inset, a necessity if the cook's repertoire includes perfect pastry. Around the corner more work tops lead to the sink unit.

The old-fashioned scrubbed wooden table provides a delightful eating place, next to the large window which makes this a lovely kitchen to live and work in — with a view of the garden. Stripped Windsor chairs are comfortable and in character with the custom-made pine cupboards, with their bright brass handles.

The beautiful old brick floor is the original one, but it has been relaid to provide an even surface. Patterned blue and white ceramic tiles provide not only a welcome touch of pattern and colour but also perhaps the most hardwearing and easy to clean of all wall surfaces. The wooden batten which edges the tiles is used for hanging kitchen tools and a picturesque string of onions.

On the right of the picture (above) this batten is topped by a narrow shelf for storing spice jars.

Decoration is important in a kitchen of this kind. It comes with the two pot plants, a painting on the wall and the old-fashioned brass scales, which are useful as well as being most attractive.

The lesson of this kitchen is that, provided the basic rules of kitchen planning are followed, there is no limit to the expression of personal taste and ideas, and materials can be borrowed from any century.

Above left: a slab of marble set in a pine work surface makes a useful pastry board Above: white walls, the black and white range and splash-back tiles make a striking contrast to the muted colours of the floor and furniture

You step up to sit at a breakfast bar with a view, turning your back on the working kitchen — which is a neat, well-fitted galley

This luxury kitchen on a small scale is a simple galley type — with one wall flanked by a working surface to accommodate the electric equipment such as toaster, mixer, blender; the eye-level fridge, and wall mounted cupboards. On the other wall, the essential elements of the kitchen follow in logical sequence: oven, work top, sink and drainer. Because the cooker is well away from the window, a powerful overhead extractor hood has been fitted to deal with cooking smells and steam.

The kitchen door is a sliding door, so as not to impinge on the work surface. Or alternatively it could be hinged to open outwards.

Overhead lighting, supplemented by a strip above the cooker, is quite sufficient in this small area, where a white-painted ceiling bounces back the light.

The dining bay has wall-mounted lights of its own, and two stools that tuck away tidily under the built-out breakfast bar.

All the surfaces in this kitchen — including the plastic stool cushions — just wipe clean . . . down to the floor, which is of attractive mock brick grey tiles.

Ideas worth adopting. The type of breakfast bar shown is the simplest to install: it is a length of wood cut to measure, supported by brackets at either end. The washing machine fits in between the oven and the sink, under the work top. It is on castors, so that it can be pulled out for use and the area behind it can be cleaned. Manoeuvrability of bulky equipment is always a good idea in the kitchen.

Camera Press

Floor plan of the kitchen

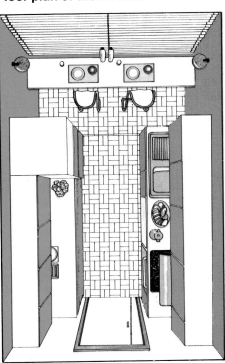

KITCHEN ON A MINIMUM SCALE

An L-shape rather than a U-shape is the only answer in this small square room, and the horizontal stripes on floor and wall make it seem larger

It's only 6 ft. 6 in. by 6 ft. 6 in. (about 2 metres by 2 metres), but it all fits in! Instead of putting the sink in the traditional position under the window, this has been reserved for the cooker — thus giving a natural ventilation outlet for the cooking smells. The fridge is next to the cooker, tucked under a working surface that runs round both sides of the L-shape of the room.

Dishes can be stacked to dry on the left of the sink. There are cupboards for crockery and pans underneath the sink, and a hole for trays next to the fridge. The two cupboards on the wall above the sink have been made slightly shorter to give ample head room. The splash-back is easy-clean tiling, and the floor lino squares.

There is no washing machine in this kitchen — but it would be possible to accommodate one by housing the fridge in the eye-level cupboard on the left of the sink, and plumbing in a front-opening washing machine next to the cooker.

Ideas worth adopting. Here, there is a table large enough for one, that pulls out from one of the storage units. An alternative would be to put a flap-up table with hinges on the wall facing the long side of the 'L'. Stacking stools are a sensible form of seating when space is at a premium, as it is here.

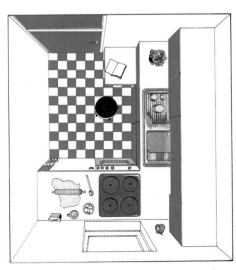

23

KITCHEN WITH ULTRA-FEMININE APPEAL

12

Soft colours and pretty accessories give a luxury look that belies the cost of fitting out this kitchen, which was built with whitewood units

You might not believe it, but this enchanting and cool looking kitchen started life as an old coal cellar! The owners extended it into the front garden, and have had the earth pushed right back to allow more light in.

Another major part of the initial conversion was to gain height for the room by digging down a couple of feet. This means the room has a totally new floor of blue and white vinyl tiles, laid in groups of four in each colour for an unusual, large chequered effect.

The pretty blue and white wallpaper sets the mood and the colour scheme, and is echoed in a strip of matching fabric used as a border in the plain blue curtains.

This kitchen is full of ideas. The expensive looking fitments are actually whitewood ones with no backs. The owners have used decorative mouldings on the doors and pretty brass knobs and handles, all of which give the kitchen a luxury look on a budget.

Lighting is a judicious mixture of old and new — strip lights under wall cupboards and over built-in shelves; a spotlight with a fringed shade to light the hobs and adjoining work surface; an old oil lamp converted to electricity that looks very decorative and can be used on the pine dining room table.

The kitchen has a sound working plan. The sink is under the window with a built-out work top adjacent to it, the dishwasher conveniently fitted underneath. The cooker hotplates come next, set into a work top, and a continuation of this work top leads to the eye-level built-in oven.

The dining end is furnished entirely with stripped pine furniture and includes a small, pretty dresser, an oval table and pine chairs upholstered in sky blue. An unusual wooden see-through screen is used to divide the two rooms without cutting them off from each other.

The whole effect is one of comfort and luxury, achieved with good taste and imagination.

Certainly the actual conversion must have been expensive, but the owners have gained a beautiful kitchen and a dining room, which is cheaper than building on or moving house.

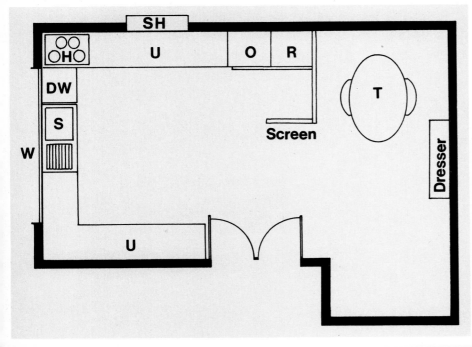

On facing page: the painted wooden screen to the right of the picture is used to cut off the dining end. On this page: a 19th century oil lamp converted to electricity makes a decorative table light. At foot: plan of kitchen

Fold-away breakfast table and stacking chairs are just two of the space-saving factors. The cupboards are cleverly fitted to provide maximum storage

BUILT-IN IDEAS IN A COMPACT KITCHEN

The kitchen shown on the previous page is full of tricks and tips for making the most of space. It is decorated in cool smart colours and natural wood. The design is an L-shape on two walls, leaving the third wall to accommodate a folding laminate-surfaced table, and a pair of matching·folding chairs, painted white. Both chairs and table shown here can be wiped clean and are a sensible size. All too often, flap-up tables are too narrow to take food for two; a minimum width should be 2 ft. 6 in. (762 mm.).

The work sequence of the kitchen is: oven and hob; space for food preparation (or serving); sink; fridge. The hob is set in a steel plate that is extended to an extra $11\frac{3}{4}$ in. (300 mm.) width in the adjacent work top to take pots and pans straight out of the oven.

The walls are a mixture of washable paint and hardwood timber panelling specially sealed against damp and stains and capable of withstanding intense heat. This is an important point to remember where, as is the case here, the panelling runs behind the burners.

A white roller blind, made from a fire-proof fabric, takes up less space and does not trap the dust as curtains would.

Particular features of this kitchen are the broom cupboard (see close-up showing built-in fitments); a special socket fitted on the front of the electric cooker for plugging in mixer, blender and other electrical equipment; a swing-out shelf with a cutter and slicer attached which is fitted in the unit on the far left, under the window.

Ideas worth adopting. The decoration scheme is exemplary: a successful blending of traditional natural wood table, chairs and panelling with the modern streamlined kitchen equipment, set in a highly sophisticated colour scheme. The whole kitchen is basically decorated in cream and white, with soft dull green high on the walls to echo the green of the trees outside the window. A polished stainless steel light fitting provides light at the right height over the folding table and looks very good against the light wood.

Above: somewhere to sit down in the kitchen and a table for the housewife to write shopping lists, consult recipe books and so on are assets. To save space in this kitchen (shown in full on the previous page), the designer allowed for a table hinged to the wall that can be shut down when not in use, and two comfortable chairs that can be folded and stacked away against the wall. This area doubles as a conveniently placed breakfast bar — one step only from the hob, cooker and sink

Left: a broom cupboard is something that's often overlooked in a kitchen. Here the cupboard has been fitted with plastic racks and hooks on the inside. There is room for furniture polish, dusters, cleaning agents, dustpan and brush, vacuum cleaner and broom. In this tidy lay-out everything is instantly to hand

Camera Press

KITCHEN THAT'S A LABOUR-SAVER

14

The working area — incorporating every gadget — has been deliberately grouped in the centre of a large room to cut down on wasteful floor space

Long, white serving hatch above a single sink slides back to connect the kitchen with the dining room. See other views of this kitchen overleaf

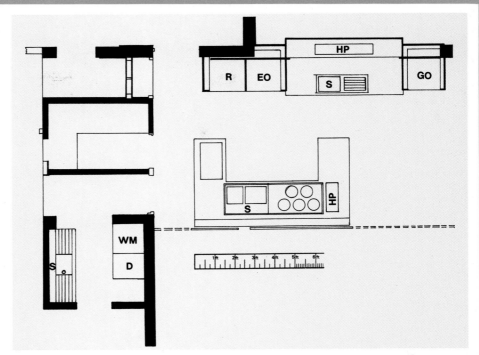

KITCHEN THAT'S A LABOUR-SAVER

The designers of this kitchen have thought of everything, beginning with clever grouping of the main work area in the centre of the room.

The concept illustrated is one of the golden rules of kitchen planning — to cut down the floor space and group all the kitchen components close together and in a logical order.

The E-shaped unit (without the centre stroke) houses the cooker hob next to a double sink. The two arms of the E form work tops, covered in heat-proof quarry tiles, with a marble slab let into one of them for pastry-making. Above the sink is a row of cupboards, one of which pulls out to reveal a cooker hood, with a built-in extractor fan and light. Under the cupboards there is hanging room for utensils and small open shelves as well as strip lights.

Another fitment just across the room houses a single sink, with a waste disposer, two ovens and a large fridge with a freezer unit at the top. Near the sink is a built-in dishwasher, and above it a long white hatch which links with the dining room. On the dining side of the hatch is a quarry-tiled work top, with an electric hot plate sunk into it to keep dishes hot in transit. The dirty dishes are then passed back, the scrapings dropped into the waste-disposer and the dishes stacked into the dishwasher.

One end of the room beyond the work area has a table and chairs for breakfast and informal family meals. A sliding door leads into the sitting room. At the other end of the kitchen a door in the panelled wall leads into a walk-in larder with wine racks built high on the wall. No space is wasted and drawers are built into the panelled wall. Well framed fruit and flower prints add a colourful note to the panelling.

Refinements of comfort include a pull-out trolley which, when not in use, looks just like a kitchen cupboard; a wall telephone, and a couple of gas rings, just in case the electricity supply should fail!

The colour scheme is simple. All the units are in warm wood finish, the floor is white vinyl (and covers under floor heating) and the richly coloured quarry tiles on the work surfaces add a warm

touch. This is a labour-saving kitchen which totally avoids looking clinical.

Ideas worth adopting: the quarry-tiled work tops, very practical and indestructible, and not an extravagance for small areas; the use of a trolley in the kitchen — perhaps not built into an expensive fitment, but just slipped out of the way under a work top; the space-saving wall telephone — a very good place to have a second telephone in the house; the marble slab for pastry — it is still possible to buy marble slabs quite cheaply in junk shops and a home handyman could set it into a work top himself.

Above: a wood-panelled door, with framed prints hung on it, leads to a capacious larder. When closed, it looks like part of the wall. The floor plan of this kitchen is shown on previous page.

Left: quarry tiles have been used as a working surface to give a warm-looking finish that's durable and easy to clean

KITCHEN THAT EXPRESSES REAL FLAIR

15

Brian Morris

**The designer made the most
of the bay window,
in what used to be a
drawing room, by placing
the bulk of the units
within the bay**

Fun is the word that springs to mind on first looking at this highly original and well designed kitchen. Crisp black and white form the basis, and colourful straw bags and kitchen utensils hang from the pine ceiling to give almost a touch of carnival. . . .

This large and comfortable kitchen used to be the drawing room of the house, and the designer, Elizabeth Meacock, made the most of the beautiful bay window by building in the kitchen fitments all round it. Most of the work in the kitchen goes on round the window, as that is where the sink and hotplates are.

The well designed storage space makes use of every nook and cranny, and follows the shape of the walls. It starts just under the ceiling, which was lowered with pine planking to improve the proportions of the room.

The room is big enough to allow a laundry corner (at the right of the picture), away from the main work flow of the kitchen. The comfortable pine table in the centre of the room goes beautifully with the smart black chairs and provides an extra work surface as well as a dining area.

Between the built-in oven and the hotplates, open shelves hold spice jars and other things in daily use. But the most unusual features in the room are round the window — pretty scalloped roller blinds and short café curtains in red and white gingham hung on a brass rod at eye level. Another rod spans the bay window much higher up and from this hang colourful straw bags. Bright enamel kitchen utensils are looped irregularly from the pine ceiling on meat hooks and add a decorative note.

Converted wall oil lamps provide light at intervals, and a brass spotlight is angled on to the dining table.

This is a splendid kitchen to work in, bright and airy, with plenty of space in the centre of the room — and just the right zany note to give an air of informality.

**Below: floor plan
of the kitchen**

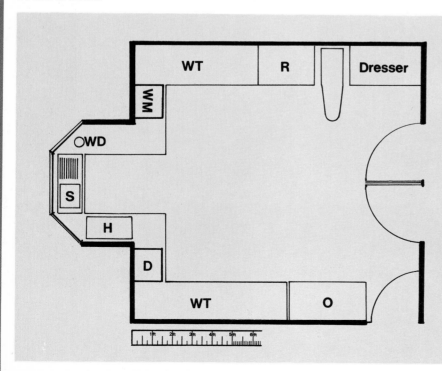

HERE STORAGE IS THE STORY

16 Two pull-out work tops combined with ingenious storage ideas have practically doubled the usable space in this attractive timber-faced kitchen

In this kitchen, every picture tells a storage story! The room was planned to a space-saving design, using every available inch for work surface and storage.

The kitchen is designed in a conventional U form. On the right wall, a set of four burners sits under an extractor hood, separated from the sink by a useful working surface. A front-opening dishwasher fits exactly under this work top.

The far end of the U form (see picture overleaf) is a continuous working surface under broad windows, above three separate storage drawers and cupboards. One of these houses two plastic vegetable racks, another holds built-in shelves for storing dry foods, and the third has triangular swivel-mounted trays to take large items.

The left-hand wall of the U holds the eye-level oven, storage cupboard

Below left: a continuous work surface runs round the perimeter of the kitchen. Even the fridge/freezer (top right corner of the picture) has been raised clear of the work surface to allow storage or preparation space below

Below right: the cupboards have been excellently fitted out with storage equipment — such as the four wooden spice holders on the inside of the high cupboard door and the plastic crockery trays built into the unit below the cooking hob. See overleaf a view of the far end of this kitchen, and a floor plan

Camera Press

HERE STORAGE IS THE STORY

16

Above: the far end
of the kitchen has windows
extending the width of the wall
to allow maximum light.
The cupboard on the left houses
two swivel trays
for carrying large items
such as teapots and mixing bowls;

the centre cupboard stores
dry foods on built-in shelves,
the right-hand cupboard has
two plastic racks for vegetables

Below: floor plan
of the kitchen shown here
and on the previous page

units above and below the washing surface, and a pull-out table to eat off or use for working.

The freezer/fridge is also on this wall, mounted at eye (and hand) level, and leaving either work or storage space clear beneath it. One of the units here has been specially adapted and fitted with a separate double power socket to house blender, mixer or other household equipment. This is an idea that could be copied in any kitchen with a cupboard or shelf to spare. Similarly, if you are starting from scratch, it is possible to have power sockets set into the side of kitchen units.

The decor of the kitchen has been restricted to three colours — green, white and brown — for smartness and simplicity.

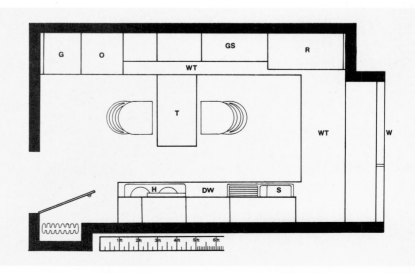

This kitchen started life as part of the standard-fitted equipment in a four-bedroom house on an estate. But the builders had enough imagination to present prospective buyers with a choice — a package deal of standard units to a certain value, or a few extras in exchange for one or two of the standard units. The owners of this kitchen opted for the latter course, and it has given them a more versatile kitchen adapted to their needs.

The most unusual part of the kitchen is the breakfast bar, which also acts as a partial room divider between the cooking and the eating ends of the room. The 'bar' is just a built-in base unit, with an L-shaped overhanging ledge running round two sides of it. The base unit is accessible for storage from the kitchen side, and

its positioning between the two long windows makes the most of daylight and uses up a 'dead' wall. Making a breakfast bar is such a good space-saving idea that handymen might like to build one for the family from the designs overleaf.

The rest of the kitchen shown here is simply but well planned with a dishwasher tucked under a work top adjoining the sink, and a split level cooker with the hob next to the waist-level oven.

The paper lantern is a good idea — cheap enough to be virtually disposable. When it's dirty or you're tired of the colour, you just buy another one. The blue tiles on the wall and the neutral coloured floor tiles are easy to maintain, and make a good background for the pink lampshade and the pink and mustard blinds.

PERSONALITY IN A STANDARD KITCHEN 17

The breakfast bar gives this simple kitchen character and acts as a partial room divider. You could build a bar yourself from the instructions overleaf

Good Housekeeping

PERSONALITY IN A STANDARD KITCHEN 17

Instructions to make the kind of breakfast bar shown on the previous page and two alternative versions.

A. The breakfast bar shown on the previous page is fairly simple for the do-it-yourself enthusiast to make. A framework of 'three by one' (or metric equivalent) timber cut to fit a standard kitchen unit is joined by screwed and glued corner blocks and then screwed to the unit or vice versa (screw the thinner material to the thicker). A top of blockboard is then cut to fit the frame and is attached with glue and screws to the frame. Laminate sheeting is cut to fit the top, then glued with an impact adhesive. This is followed by cutting and glueing the side pieces, and filing down to form a neat finish where the edges butt.

If you want to use ready-faced laminated boarding, this can be attached by screwing through blocks or brackets attached to the underside of the frame. The timber left

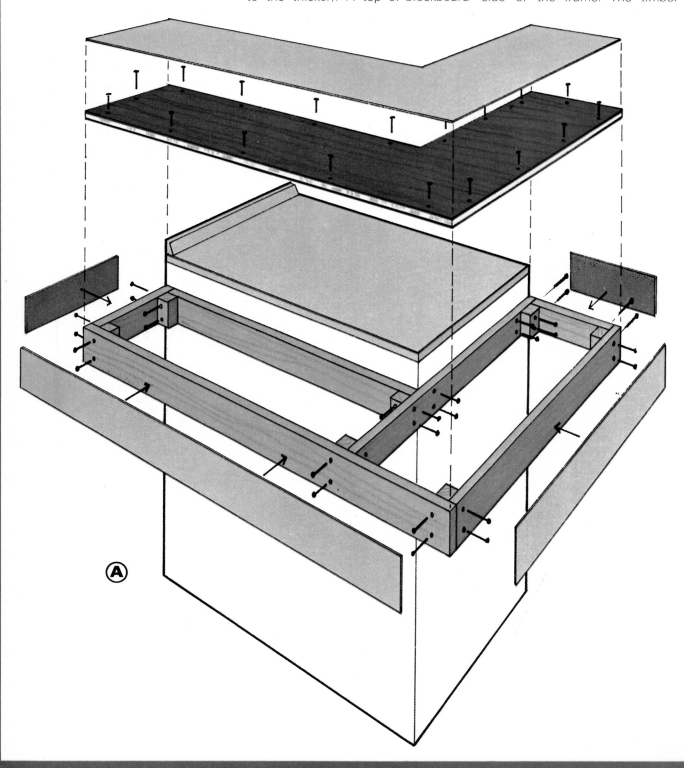

Ⓐ

38

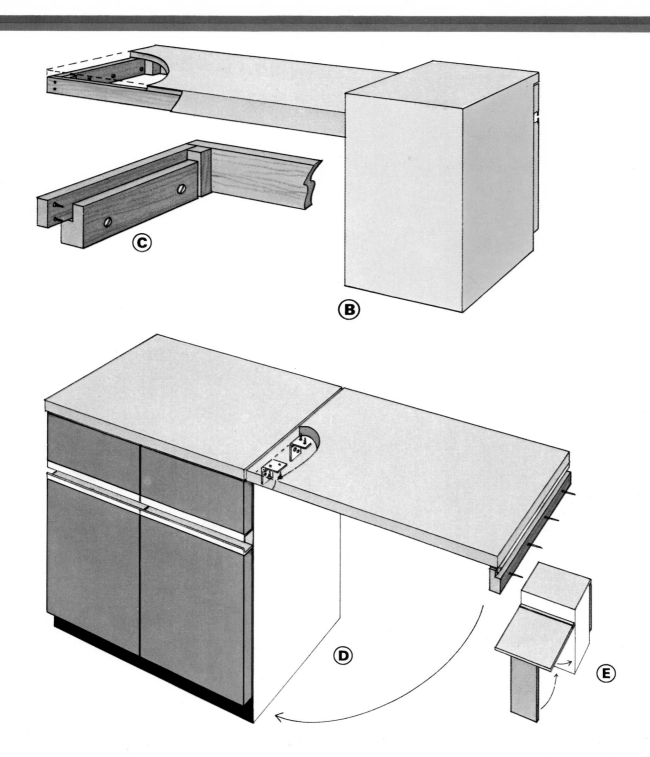

C

B

D

E

exposed is then covered with matching laminate.

B. If you have room in your kitchen, it is easy to use a unit and a simple breakfast bar. Using the same framing technique as the drawing on the facing page, the bench is simply screwed to the wall at one end and to the unit at the other. Set the top of the bench at about 28 inches (71 mm.), so you can use ordinary chairs. If you were to set the bench at the full height of the unit you would have to use high stools.

C. The detail drawing shows a way of

using this bench top as an occasional table by fitting a block of timber to the wall and a corresponding block on the unit. The wall block has been cut to form a stand-up lip which allows the end frame (in this instance made from shallower timber) to rest on it.

The bar can be lifted off when not required.

D. An alternative way of building a bench for occasional use is to make a hinged top to attach to the side of a free-standing unit. The length of the top must be shorter than the

depth of the unit by the thickness of the timber used to make the top. A length of L-angled aluminium is screwed to the underside of the top, on the edge to be lifted up, and this fits into a channel cut in the timber screwed to the wall. When the top is lifted, the unit must be moved an inch so as to allow the angle strip to settle into its channel.

E. A further variation on this idea is to put a flap on the end of the top, to use as a leg. The flap must be shorter than the top, to fold away when not in use.

KITCHEN WITH A DREAMY QUALITY 18

Dramatic lighting
distinguishes this
open-plan kitchen and
breakfast bar, designed
in two L shapes and linking
with the living area

This beautiful kitchen has what can only be described as star quality. Basically open plan with the dining and living area adjoining, the kitchen is ingeniously designed as two L-shaped units. One houses the working area; the other forms the wood-topped breakfast bar.

All the equipment is built in to give a tidy look, so essential in any open plan kitchen, and no space has been wasted. There are cupboards under the whole of the breakfast bar on the kitchen side. The decor links both areas — the bar is faced with wood, echoing the colour of the lovely hard wood floor in the dining area.

This kitchen in a large modern family house has been designed as the heart of the home. It is open to the whole of the living area and easily accessible to the five children in the family who have their bedrooms and bathroom grouped near the kitchen.

The owners say the roomy breakfast bar has proved so useful that the family usually use the dining area only when they are entertaining. The bar stools with upholstered seats have backs for extra comfort.

The actual working area is simple and compact. It includes a broom cupboard, a family-size refrigerator, a double oven and a rotisserie built in at eye level. Also, there are four hot plates, placed under an extractor hood. The double sink has a waste-disposal unit and is built under the handsome sliding windows which take up the whole of one kitchen wall.

Extra luxuries are a built-in food mixer and a telephone on the breakfast bar.

The kitchen floor is covered with practical vinyl tiles, and the bar top is sealed to make it spill-proof.

The lighting is one of the chief charms of this kitchen. The handsome red glass pendant lights provide a dramatic decorative feature, as well as bright light over the breakfast bar. They are also a visual divider between the kitchen and the dining end.

Ideas worth adopting. The simple idea of using two L shapes — one for the working kitchen, another for a breakfast bar — could be followed less ambitiously, using cheaper materials and a standard range of kitchen units.

Below: floor plan of the kitchen

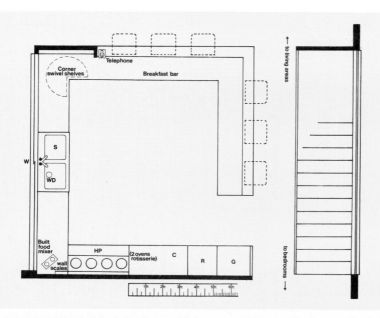

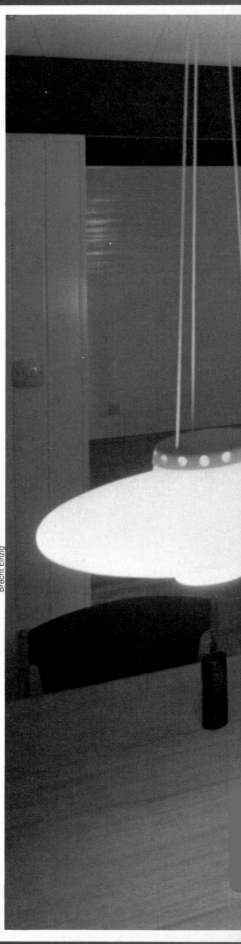

Brecht Einzig

KITCHEN WITH A CENTRAL BONUS

The built-in island unit houses burners and cupboards, doubles as a breakfast bar and cuts down walking in this kitchen

One of the best ways of putting value-less floor space to good use in a kitchen is to build in a centre unit. However, many people will not even consider the idea, for they worry that it will take up too much room. The easiest way to decide whether or not there is sufficient space is to draw a scale plan of the kitchen on graph paper showing all the fittings. If, with the addition of a centre unit, there is still enough room for two people to pass each other and to work back to back, then there is enough room for the unit.

In this kitchen, the centre unit takes the hob, and the sinks and oven are sited within easy reach. An unusual canopy with a scalloped edge sits over the hob to take away cooking odours at source. A light fitted in the canopy gives the cook direct brightness to supplement the general kitchen lighting from strips under the wall-mounted cupboards.

There is no external door, so the problem of waste disposal has been dealt with by fitting a waste-disposer in one of the twin stainless steel sinks. In addition, a concealed rubbish chute carries away the refuse to a bin outside the house.

This kitchen has been specially designed to fit into a small alcove of an overall living/dining/cooking area, and all the units were custom-built by the manufacturers. Sometimes, when the position or shape of a kitchen presents technical problems, the only answer is to call in the kitchen experts. Their design may cut down on the number of units you need to buy, and save money in the long run.

Ideas worth adopting. There is a lesson to be learnt from the effective handling of open-plan decor as shown here. Part of the dividing wall has been retained, which has the effect of framing the kitchen area. Maintaining the same colour scheme in both cooking and dining ends of the room gives a feeling of cohesion.

Grovewood

U-SHAPED AND BUDGET-CONSCIOUS 20

A classic arrangement, using the minimum of expensive equipment in the best possible sequence, successfully divides the cooking area from the dining room. The all-over colour scheme harmonises the two areas

This is a good example of simple, functional kitchen planning, using the minimum of expensive equipment. The traditional U form as shown here applies to many kitchens, whether open plan or built around three walls.

The work sequence follows a logical pattern: fridge, double stainless steel sink, work surface (on the corner where two sides of the square meet, thus giving extra depth) and cooker. To the left of the cooker is a storage

Format Mobelwerke

cupboard for pots and pans; to the right of it is a series of drawers to take the kitchen cutlery, pot holders, tea towels and so on.

One arm of the U separates the kitchen area from the dining area, doubles as a sideboard, and has fitted drawers and cupboards on both sides to house the dining room equipment as well as the kitchen.

The doors of all the units finish a little short of the floor, making it easy for the housewife to clean underneath. All work surfaces are made of tough yellow laminate; the floor is a patterned wipe-clean lino-leum that runs through both kitchen and dining areas.

Care has been taken to match the mood of the dining furniture to the kitchen equipment, so as to make the two areas blend into a harmonious whole. The gay yellow roller blinds are made from a coated fabric that can be cleaned with a damp cloth. The dark wall covering gives impact to the yellow and white furnishings and fittings, while a white ceiling makes the whole room seem higher and brighter.

It all adds up to a comfortable family kitchen, where the housewife can chat to friends who have called in or can keep an eye on the children while she goes about her cooking and cleaning.

KITCHEN MADE FOR A CAREER GIRL

21

Streamlined, well-planned units for easy working; a feature of this kitchen is the built-in shelf along the window which provides an office corner

This smart little kitchen is perfect for a working girl. It was designed around the bay window, where a long narrow ledge — just deep enough to take a typewriter, address book, and supply of paper — has been built in. A high stool tucks away under the ledge when not in use.

One wall houses twin ovens, set one on top of the other, next door to the burners. A built-in canopy extracts food smells, and is fitted with a light to illuminate the cooking area.

To the right of the ovens, an awkwardly shaped space has been put to good use by making small open shelves to house storage jars. And, under the

Vivienne Hislop

shelves, a pull-out rail has been fitted for drying damp tea towels.

Facing the cooking hob and ovens, two units have been placed together in an L-shape. The short area of the L is a peninsular unit which offers storage space and a breakfast bar; the other longer unit holds a double stainless steel sink.

The ovens, hob, sinks and working surfaces are all within a few paces of one another, making this an easy kitchen to work in. The large fridge/ freezer (in the extreme lefthand corner) has been kept out of the way of the cooking area, but is next to the peninsular unit for easy loading.

Ideas worth adopting. A special leaf can be taken out of the decorator's notebook here. The colour scheme is a smart red, white and grey-green, but given a warm touch by using a floral print of red, green, blue and yellow on the roller blind. For a window of this size, a blind looks neat and has the virtue of being cheaper to make than curtains, since it needs considerably less fabric.

A coat of quick-drying red lacquer on accessories such as the tray and tea pot to match the red wall tiles puts the finishing touch to this stream-lined kitchen.
Right: floor plan of the kitchen

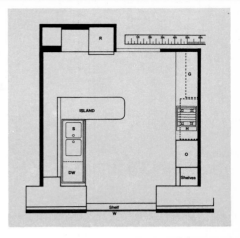

KITCHEN 22 THAT'S CAST IN TIMBER

Wood makes a warm and practical surface for the walls and ceiling of this kitchen, built on the upper floor to make the most of a fabulous view

This is an upstairs kitchen, part of the first floor of a house that's deep in the country. The view would delight any housewife chained to the sink — which has been placed deliberately under the window. The whole of the upper floor, including the kitchen, is constructed of timber and supported by the old stone walls of an existing cottage.

Wood is particularly vulnerable to damp and staining, so the timber walls of the kitchen have been sealed to give them protection and make them washable. The wooden frames and beams are all finished with a black preservative.

The units were purpose-made to fit the shape of the room, but it would be possible to use cheaper whitewood models and surface them yourself with laminate. A hatch cover, set in the work surface next to the cooker, gives access to the refuse chute. This takes the rubbish straight down into the bin.

Sturdy open shelves house a quantity of glass jars containing items such as sugar, coffee and tea. Architect Graham Brooks, who designed this kitchen for his own house, says that the jars have a double value. They are not only decorative but useful — since you can see at a glance when supplies are running low.

The double sink unit has one small bowl (good for preparing vegetables) and another larger one. There is space on the adjoining work surface for a plastic plate drainer.

Ideas worth adopting. Few kitchens are upstairs, as this is. But even on the ground floor, giving the housewife a view of the outside world — if only of the back garden — while she is at work at the sink is the kind of bonus that makes for human contentment in the kitchen.

Sam Lambert

IT'S TWICE AS LONG AS IT'S DEEP

23

But clever design has
overcome an awkward shape.
Building in a breakfast
table and matching
banquettes greatly improves
the proportions of the room

Neat as a new pin and so handsomely
designed, this kitchen earns its position
in the open plan of an attractive
modern house. Access to the kitchen
is easy and a hatch at the right of the
breakfast corner leads to the dining
room. Light pours in through the glass
wall which looks on to the patio and
one of the windows nearest the kitchen
is fitted with glass louvres to help
ventilation.

The whole effect is one of sophisti-
cation with the oiled teak used for
work tops and door frames set off by
black and white laminated facings.
Black is also used for upholstering the
banquettes in the breakfast corner, and
a handsome stainless steel cooker
hood (designed by the architect who
built the house) efficiently disposes of
cooking smells.

Glazed brown ceramic tiles with an
embossed pattern make an expensive
but very hard-wearing floor that is
child's play to keep clean. The tiles
are used for the whole corridor, leading
the eye gently into the living area
beyond, carpeted in a toning brown.

The walls are white, and the ceiling
comprises wooden slats with lights
inset. A low light over the breakfast
corner is diffused from a brass
coloured fitment. A practical aid is
provided by the inset of heat-proof
tiles next to the cooker hob which will
take kindly to spills and splashes. A
double fridge and deep freeze and oven
are built in on the facing wall; the sink
is on the wall just out of view in these
pictures.

Idea worth adopting: the space-
saving and very attractive breakfast
corner, perhaps neater than a free-
standing table and chairs. This could
be copied fairly inexpensively, as
banquettes can be bought and could
be built in by a home handyman.

Sam Lambert

ELEGANT TOUCHES IN A WELL-KNIT KITCHEN 24

The sleek colour scheme and the copper and china on display give a living room quality to this kitchen, laid out to save the housewife time and motion

Elizabeth Ann

This kitchen has been carefully planned to put the three main elements — oven, hob and sink — within a few paces of each other. Each is surrounded by a continuous working surface.

There is a hatch through to the dining room, cut in the wall next to the eye-level oven, with ample shelf space for serving meals. Underneath have been fitted the fridge, one fixed storage unit and a second unit on castors that can be wheeled out to double as a drinks trolley.

The floor and splash-backs above the hob and sink have been lined with patterned tiles that match; the walls have been painted olive green to blend with the green and woodgrain finish of the units. Instead of curtains, attractive white-painted louvres have been set in the window frame.

A peninsular unit that stretches across half the width of the kitchen gives valuable storage space (with door access on both sides) and cuts off a corner for the housewife to work in. Her 'desk' is a broad shelf, supported by brackets, built on the side of the unit. A hanging lamp, set low, gives plenty of light; a tall stool is just the right height to sit on and uses up little space.

Ideas worth adopting. The row of kitchen tools, the wooden salt box, clock, calendar and telephone have all been fixed to the wall where they are easily accessible but cannot be knocked over.

A working corner is invaluable to all housewives, preferably kept clear of the cooking area; if space is at a premium, the desk could be a pull-out flap or hinged shelf.

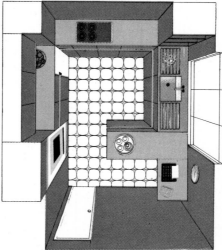

**Above: a spotlight over the hob, a spotlight over the sink and a spotlight over the housewife's desk corner supplement the strip lighting under the wall cupboards
Right: the housewife's desk corner is in a little-used area of the room, with wall-mounted clock, telephone and calendar put where they will be of most use
Above right: louvre shutters that fold back during the day give this kitchen a living room ambience
Far right: the dining hatch is in a key position next to the cooker and above the fridge. Food can be served straight through to the dining table**

KITCHEN IN AN ATTIC FLAT 25

Everything has been designed to lead the eye to this room's built-in bonus — the flower-filled roof garden, which is just a step or two away from the sink

This cool and pretty kitchen is part of a small flat at the top of an office block and has the advantage of opening straight on to a roof garden.

The crisp blue and white decor is a marvellous foil for the garden, which catches the eye as soon as one enters the kitchen. The warm cork floor (sealed to avoid staining, as cork is an absorbent material) echoes the terracotta of the flower pots; the white fitments pick up the white of the table and chairs outside.

All the units are custom-built with practical laminated surfaces and, though the kitchen is not large, it is planned to make working in it easy and pleasant.

The storage fitment on the left of the picture provides a large work surface, next to the cooker; another work top links the cooker to the stainless steel sink. There is ample storage space in the wall and floor cupboards and the large fridge across the room is easy to get to and does not impede the traffic flow.

An extractor fan is fitted above the cupboards, an important point in a small kitchen with an integral dining end. The unusual tiered cane basket makes a decorative and space-saving way to store vegetables.

Ideas worth adopting. The checked blue blind (see plan) which is home-made, can be drawn over the glass door at night without any impediment to the view of the garden during day-time. Another feature of the kitchen (not shown) is a wall of louvre-drape blinds which can be pulled down to divide the kitchen from the dining area at the other end.

The pretty dining room is carpeted in the same shade of blue as the kitchen, and has white walls and a white table and chairs.

Elizabeth Whiting

Floor plan of the kitchen and dining room

54

HEART OF THE HOME

Does that mean that the kitchen — even if quite small — should serve as a family centre as well as a food preparation centre?

'Once you put a woman into one of our kitchens you just can't get her out again.' This has been the slogan for a range of glossy fitted kitchens. Whatever the validity of the manufacturer's claim, most housewives *do* spend a large part of their working day in the kitchen. How much will depend on the size and demands of the family, how ambitious a cook the wife is and the size and type of kitchen she has inherited or planned for herself.

A great deal of the business of homemaking goes on in kitchens. Food is stored there — both on a day-to-day and long-term basis. Meals are prepared and cooked, the utensils washed up and the debris collected and thrown out or disposed of. Cutlery and crockery may have to be stored, as well as pots and pans and cooking utensils.

If the kitchen is large enough, family meals — certainly breakfast — will be eaten there, and it may be the family's laundry room as well, with a corner for the weekly ironing.

A fairly capacious, comfortable, warm and pleasant kitchen can become the centre of the family's activities and double as a second living room. In this case a large table is an essential. After supper, it could be cleared for the children's homework, leaving the parents the sole use of the living area. The housewife who makes her own clothes could use it for cutting out the patterns — and what better place for sewing large items, like curtains?

Kitchens have been the scene of some of the best children's parties. There's not too much worry about spills on the floor or fingermarks on the walls. There's an easy supply line to nursery delicacies like sausages hot from the oven and trifles, jellies and ice cream out of the fridge.

In case this sounds like a homely, haphazard haven, remember that careful use of space is as important in a large kitchen as in a small one. In a small kitchen you must plot every inch, to make the most of what you've got. In a large kitchen you must design the area to avoid having to walk miles in a working week.

'Divide and rule' should be the slogan for the large kitchen. Make the working part of the kitchen as small as possible, with everything grouped within easy reach — the fridge, the cooker, the sink, cupboards and work tops.

Adoption of the 'island' principle helps. The working area is concentrated in the centre of the room. It incorporates the sink and hotplates and enough space is left for a breakfast bar. An effective example of an island kitchen shown in this book is 'Kitchen with a Central Bonus'. Or the kitchen can be divided into dining end and a working end, the latter embraced by an E-shaped fitment (without the centre arm). An example in these pages is 'Kitchen that's a Labour-saver'. In both these cases, storage space and work tops have been wisely increased at the expense of floor or walking area.

If you want to live in your kitchen, do not make it too clinical. A few pieces of old furniture will blend surprisingly well with modern fitted units — and probably keep costs down. In recent years, there has been something of a swing away from the purely functional kitchen and many traditional materials back in favour are very practical for kitchen use. Wood, properly sealed with two or three coats of clear polyurethane sealer, makes a wonderful wall covering. It looks warm, can be wiped clean and cuts down on decorating. The dining end of a predominantly timber kitchen can be furnished with stripped pine furniture; the table can be scrubbed, the chairs just wiped with a damp cloth. Other traditional materials like quarry tiles — or even old floor bricks — are easy to keep clean (but in a cold kitchen they do strike a chill first thing in the morning), while patterned ceramic tiles are an expensive but virtually indestructible form of wall-covering and decoration.

Roller blinds in bright colours, or prettily patterned, contribute a living room look to the kitchen and make the most of light when completely rolled up. Curtains tend to rob light. They also get in the way of the busy cook, and absorb dust and grease. Like roller blinds, small areas of patterned, washable paper add personality. Many washable wallpapers have a matching fabric. You could have a blind made up in the fabric and perhaps add a table cloth for the dining area.

A portable radio is a great morale-booster for the housewife in the kitchen. So is a telephone extension that enables her to talk to her friends without risk of the milk boiling over. Small but important extras include a wall clock, somewhere to store cookery books, and a slate or pad and pencil for family messages, shopping lists and reminders of what in the store cupboard needs replenishing.

So much for kitchens large enough to live in. What of the housewives who are stuck with really small kitchens? They are not necessarily at a disadvantage. Even a tiny kitchen can work beautifully if it's well planned. Within a small kitchen the housewife has everything almost at her fingertips and need move only a few paces in the process of preparing food, cooking and washing up. But the working sequence in a small kitchen is vital, especially if it is also to be lived in to the extent that the wife and her husband can perch on stools to eat a scratch meal. Re-positioning existing units may be necessary to give extra work tops and more storage space. The insides of doors can be used for storage with plastic-covered wire shelves, or to house a dustbin unit with disposable bags. The perhaps obvious trick of using cuphooks under cupboards and inside fitments to hang things on will leave vital shelf space for bulkier items.

Even if the room is miniscule, breakfast in the kitchen makes a lot of sense. It saves time and motion at a time of day that for many people is not the brightest. Cooked breakfasts can be served piping hot from the stove and dishes washed up on the spot. With a little forethought a breakfast corner can be introduced into the tiniest kitchen, even if it is only a pull-out flap (see 'Kitchen that's a Bachelor's Delight'). Stools can be slid under counters when not in use and the breakfast bar becomes just another useful work top.

Making a small kitchen the 'heart of the home' — where the family can eat their meals and relax — demands ingenuity. A larger kitchen can obviously serve the purpose more easily. Even here, it's as well to adopt physical possibilities to human likes and dislikes.

A team of sociologists investigating the relationship of the kitchen to family life questioned a random sample of families. The responses were intriguing.

One husband said he loathed having breakfast at the breakfast bar in the kitchen, let alone the evening meal, because the sight of the sink a few yards away induced in him a guilt complex about washing up. A family with a really enormous divided kitchen where they gave quite formal dinner parties at the non-working end abandoned the custom for a similar reason; it dawned on them that the stacks of washing up accumulating at the working end as a festive evening wore on became an acute embarrassment to their guests.

Many of the respondents in this survey said the sights, sounds and smells of cooking dulled rather than whetted their appetites. Several housewives said they disliked being under scrutiny while preparing food or clearing away, a reaction underlining the adage that no woman can share a kitchen with another — perhaps not even with her husband and children. One woman said she felt a kitchen was an intimate place and that if any strangers opened her refrigerator door she felt as though they were probing in her desk; after all, she said, the contents of the fridge were as good an indicator as any of her family's budget. She would not dream of inviting any but her closest intimates into the kitchen. As for asking party guests into the kitchen to help themselves from a cold buffet, the thought repelled her.

The survey also brought to light counter-balancing affirmations of the kitchen as a good place to live in as well as to prepare food in. First, if the family have their domestic being in the kitchen — eating and conversing there, perhaps even doing the paper work (whether office leftovers or children's homework) — the 'official' living room is kept in a pristine state from one day to another. Thus, one room to clear up and clean instead of two. Second, many stay-at-home women, cut off from human contact for most of the day, welcome the family around them in the evenings and at week-ends when they are preparing meals. 'Come and talk to me', they say, hoping the appeal is heard in the living room.

Not every family wants to live in the kitchen — beyond sharing rushed breakfasts or rummaging in the fridge after a night out. There are perfectly contented households where meals are meeting points and everybody then prefers to go his or her private way. There are others where the logical place for the television set — that other new major family meeting point — is certainly in the kitchen.

All of which emphasises the need to decide exactly what you require of your kitchen — food centre only, or food centre plus domestic social centre — before you arrange and equip it.

Juliet Wilson

KITCHEN OF THE FUTURE

This revolutionary design,
including a built-in
computer as a
desirable extra,
could be the forerunner
of the ideal kitchen
of the future

John Prizeman

In the last 40 years, machines that great grandmother could have imagined only in her wildest dreams have become normal perquisites in the kitchen . . . . dishwashers, deep freezers, self-cleaning ovens that switch themselves on and off, to mention just a few of them.

But today's housewife still has not only to think up menus and do the shopping, but measure out ingredients, blend or mix them and prepare the vegetables. After the meal is over she has to wash up or at least load and unload the dishwasher.

In another 30 or 40 years' time, will the cook have to struggle with the same chores? Perhaps not. It will be technically feasible for her lot to be greatly eased, with automation, already in its stride in the kitchen, playing an ever-increasing role as her proxy.

Discarding the wilder realms of futuristic fantasy, many leading industrial designers and architects have conducted feasibility studies to determine what is — and what is not — likely to become practicable and economic.

One of the men who has been looking ahead to the kitchen of the future is the architect, John Prizeman, who designed the revolutionary kitchen shown on these pages. It is based around three revolving units, with a computer as a desirable extra. Apart from the computer, it would be theoretically possible to install this kitchen now in your own home — if you were prepared to rip out everything in your existing kitchen and to spend a great deal of money.

The round units in the kitchen of the future were made by David Esdaile. Two of the units are short, with overhanging hoods that contain circular drums for storing dry foods. You pull down the drums, dial the amount you want and it just falls straight into your mixing bowl. The drum is then automatically restocked from above. Between them, these two units house

the sink, four hot-plates, a teak chopping board and marble pastry slab, and several storage cupboards. The tall unit holds a micro-wave oven, a self-cleaning double oven, fridge/ freezer, dishwasher and more storage space (sufficient for all the small electrical equipment).

All three units revolve slowly by hand — so the housewife can stand still and adjust the work sequence of her appliances to suit the job in hand.

The kitchen has stainless steel walls, with built-in cupboards large enough to take lesser-used equipment such as vacuum cleaners and brooms. The tops are also made of stainless steel. The floor comprises vinyl tiles in subdued greens and browns. The laminated circular units are bright orange, giving the whole kitchen a warm glow.

What are the advantages of this revolutionary design?

First, the housewife can get at every appliance with minimum effort. Second, since the units are clear of the walls, they do not suffer from the usual design limitations imposed by doors and windows . . . and there is space around the sides of the room for extra storage. Third, every single item in the kitchen is labour-saving.

Perhaps, however, the biggest advantage is the item not yet available — the computer. This will answer questions such as 'What can I give 10 guests for dinner, one of whom does not eat fish?' by flashing menus on a tiny television screen housed in the hood of one of the units, and linking this answer to a full-scale cooking demonstration projected on the kitchen wall.

Unfortunately, it is unlikely that there will be a receiving centre for the computer to translate instructions to, and receive an answer from, until this kitchen is mass-produced. So you may have to wait a while. Just as great grandmother had to wait for her dishwasher!

KITCHEN GLOSSARY

Once the grand plan has been decided, a kitchen is as effective or otherwise as its components. Here is a tactical guide to kitchen equipment, fitments and utensils

THE KITCHEN UNITS

There is an almost bewilderingly wide choice of kitchen units on the market. Buy the best you can afford.

Look for drawers which slide easily, doors which are easy to open and do not stick. Aim for a range which has a variety of sizes and shapes to allow for a flexible arrangement.

The finish of units is important; you do not want to have to paint your fitments every few years. Most units are now faced with hard-wearing plastic. If you prefer the look of natural wood, this is available in a plain or louvred finish, but make sure that it has been sealed to preserve the wood and make it easy to clean.

Look at as many makes as you can and really shop around before you decide which to buy. Sliding doors are a space-saver but make sure that they run freely on proper tracks; there is nothing more infuriating than sliding doors that jam and stick. Hinged doors come with a choice of shelves hung on the inside to provide extra storage space. The glossier ranges have trolleys which pull out and look like a floor cabinet when not in use; breakfast bars which can be fitted to peninsular units; and swing-out corner shelves for easy reaching.

The colour choice in kitchen units is greater than it has ever been, but here again think very hard before you decide. Too much colour can be tiring in a kitchen, and it may be better to choose white for the units and place colour on the walls and floor instead. Or choose a wood finish for the kitchen units and add colour in tiles, wallpaper or a pretty blind. The old chestnut that white shows the dirt should be ignored. If there is dirt in a kitchen, it is far better that you should be able to see it and get rid of it!

A number of manufacturers make a range of units ready to assemble. These are far cheaper than the ready-built ranges, but you have to be reasonably handy and, above all, you must measure the room and the fitments dead accurately or you are going to be left with gaps to fill where you don't want them.

If your kitchen happens to be in the corner of a bed-sitting room, there are inexpensive mini kitchens available.

As an example, one of these 'minis' provides a stainless steel sink, a two-plate electric cooker, a 4.8 cu. ft. refrigerator and a cupboard with extra storage in the door — all within one unit measuring $35\frac{1}{2}$ in. high by $39\frac{1}{2}$ in. wide, 24 in. deep (90.17 cm. by 100.33 cm. by 60.96 cm.).

THE SINK UNIT

It is possible that the sink unit will be the most costly item among your kitchen fitments. You have a choice between stainless steel (virtually indestructible) and vitreous enamel, which often comes in a choice of colours. Some of the more expensive kitchen ranges are only available with a stainless steel sink.

There is a good choice of sink designs. You can have a single bowl with one drainer (on its right or on its left), a double bowl with one or two drainers, or a bowl can be sunk into a work top. There are firms that make stainless steel sinks to order — to fit any design. If you are going to have a waste-disposer you must decide at this stage, as the sink needs to have a specially large drainage hole to accommodate it.

THE FLOOR

After the kitchen units, the floor is possibly the most important part of the kitchen. You want it to last a long time, as re-flooring a kitchen is a disruptive business. It must be easy to keep clean and not show every mark, or you will spend your life on your hands and knees or wielding a mop. It must not absorb fat or acid stains, and ideally it should be warm and not too hard, as one does spend a fair amount of time standing in a kitchen.

Quarry tiles are beautiful, very hard-wearing and easy to wipe clean, but they are not soft to walk on and they can be chilly in a cold kitchen.

Ceramic tiles come in glorious colours and patterns, are hard-wearing and easy to wash, but they are expensive and are best in a hot climate.

Cork, warm to walk on, soft and sound-deadening, is not, nevertheless, wholly suitable for kitchens, since it absorbs fat stains. But it can be sealed. Better still is the variety which is covered with a vinyl skin. This is, perhaps, the best of all worlds: the warmth and attractive natural look of cork with the ease of maintenance of vinyl.

Vinyl is very good for kitchen floors. But make sure you do not choose a plain colour, which will show every mark. Vinyl is available in an array of colours, patterns and qualities, some attractively designed to imitate old Provencal tiles. It comes in sheet and tile form.

Wood. Provided it has been properly sealed (three coats of special

1. Self-sticking tiles are easy to lay
2, 3 & 4. Ceramic tiles come in a colourful choice of patterns and borders
5. Best way to use a few tiles

sealer are a necessity), wood makes a good kitchen floor. It is warm, attractive to look at and, once sealed, it can be wiped clean with a damp mop.

Composition tiles and linoleum are suitable for kitchens, but make sure yours is of a sufficiently heavy gauge.

THE WALLS AND CEILING
You have the opportunity to extend beyond paint or paper.

For small areas ceramic tiles provide a tough, easy-to-clean surface that could last forever. Wood (sealed with three coats of polyurethane sealer) makes not only an attractive wall-covering but will effectively appear to lower a too-high kitchen ceiling.

The initial outlay may be heavier than for paint or paper, but the wood is there for good and you will not have to re-decorate. It is quite sensible to have one or two large walls covered in wood panelling and to have smaller areas of paint or paper, providing colour and pattern, which you can change when you get tired of the colour scheme.

Wallpaper used in a kitchen should be washable. Better still, use a vinyl paper, which is tough and washable. Paint should be oil based to withstand steam and damp.

Ceramic tiles are available in white and many plain colours and in a variety of patterns. Some are designed for the do-it-yourself market and are fairly inexpensive and simple to put up. They are ideal behind the cooker and as a splashback to the sink.

Some of the sheet vinyl used for flooring is made in scaled down patterns and can be used successfully on walls to give the kitchen a look of continuity.

Mosaic, either glass or plastic, is also good for small areas of wall. Glass mosaic is, in general, expensive and must be professionally laid. But the colours are beautiful and subtle There are do-it-yourself varieties that come in sheets and are not difficult for the amateur to put up.

THE COOKER
The basic choice for your cooker is between gas and electricity. It is possible to use bottled gas for cookers.

Some people swear by electricity; others prefer gas and a 'flame you can actually see'. Today's electric cookers are much faster than they used to be and more flexible to control. Split level cookers give the cook the choice of both fuels — for instance, an electric hob and a gas cooker, or vice versa. They also make for far greater flexibility in kitchen layout and mean less bending for the housewife. Another asset: they are safer for children, as the cooking rings can be set far back on the work tops out of reach of small hands, and the controls, too, can be built in out of the way.

The advent of the self-cleaning oven eliminates one of the nastiest chores in the housewife's repertoire. The oven, which is electric, heats up to a temperature high enough to burn anything off the interior. Solid fuel cookers have always had this ability and so have the new gas-fired versions of these old favourites. A cheaper alternative is a supply of oven liners which automatically remove whatever is splashed on to them during cooking.

But the best looking recent innovation is to do with hobs and not with ovens. This is a glass ceramic hob, with the rings merely marked on the top. No crevices, no inset rings to trap fat and food particles; just a perfectly smooth white top to wipe clean.

Some country housewives with large kitchens extol the virtues of the comforting solid fuel cookers that are now commonly considered archaic. These are now obtainable in gas-fired or oil-fired versions, doing away with cleaning and riddling. With plenty of hob space at a very good height, they are reliable cookers for large families. Most models have two ovens (self-cleaning) — one for simmering — and they can be used to supply central and water heating as well.

REFRIGERATORS AND FREEZERS
You should allow yourself as much refrigerator space as you have room for. There is nothing more irritating than juggling with plates and dishes in an attempt to fit everything into a small fridge. If you need a lot of fridge capacity and cannot accommodate a really large one, it might be better and cheaper to buy two small ones and have them built in.

Some fridges have freezers built in at the top. These are very convenient for freezing small quantities, and access to the food is easy. Chest freezers, which are suitable for large families, keep the cold air in better

than front-opening models, but the food parcels do tend to get lost in the bottom. Freezers do not have to be stored in the kitchen. Any cool place will do. The garage can sometimes serve, particularly if it has direct access to the house.

DISHWASHERS

For quite a number of families, dishwashers are still almost a luxury item. Undoubtedly they ease the housewife's tedious round of washing up. They can be free-standing or built-in. Some models will sit on a work top. Look for ease of loading and the number of place settings accommodated before you decide to buy a dishwasher. Too small a dishwasher could be of very little use in a large family or in a home where guests are frequently entertained.

HOT WATER

If you have some form of central heating, it should supply you with all the running hot water that you need in the kitchen. But if you lack central heating, you will need an independent way of heating water. This could take the form of a gas water heater near the sink. These heaters vary in size. They need an outside flue and must be serviced regularly. Electric immersion heaters are another answer.

OTHER KITCHEN NECESSITIES

Electric points should be carefully plotted in a well thought-out kitchen. The main light switch should be near the door to avoid the hazard of stumbling around in a dark kitchen.

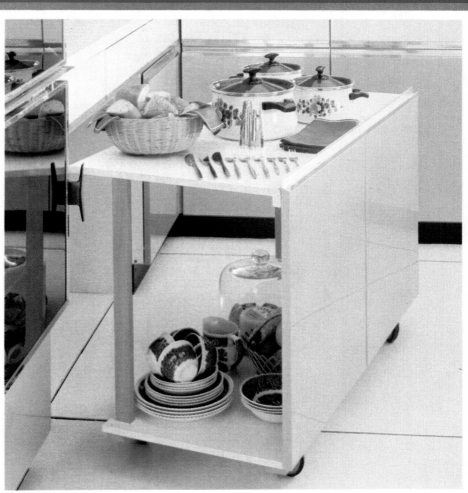

1. Space-saving waste bin unit is fixed to the inside of a cupboard door. Features include a removable inner bin and a top which fits snugly, so no smell escapes inside the cupboard
2. Two hidden assets in a cupboard; an extra work top to take the mixer and a plastic tray to hold all the attachments
3. No more scrabbling for saucepans; these swing-out shelves bring them within your reach
4. A trolley in the kitchen is invaluable, particularly when, like this one, it's designed to fit under a worktop and blend in with the cupboard doors
5. Another good way to store pots and pans – this pull-out unit has plastic-coated shelves, easy to keep clean

You may need as many as 10 electric outlet sockets to supply an electric cooker and water heater plus fridge, waste disposer, electric kettle, fan heater, blender, mixer, toaster and other accessories.

Blinds are really more practical than curtains in a kitchen. They can be rolled right up and out of the way. They will not rob the window of any light and will not absorb grease and dust during the day. Venetian blinds are very easy to keep clean and there is a large choice of colours. If you prefer something particularly feminine, choose the specially treated fabric blinds. They cannot be washed, but can be dusted and gently sponged. Patterns range from pretty floral ones to more stylised designs, bringing pattern and colour into the kitchen.

Shelves earn their keep in any kitchen. They can be fitted between wall and floor cupboards to provide storage for spice jars and other things in constant use. Housing attractive jars, they can give an otherwise clinical kitchen a cosier look. Shelves should be covered with a plastic surface for easy cleaning, or the natural wood should be sealed.

Trays are awkard objects to store flat, as normally they do not fit into standard size units. Use gaps between fitments to make room for storing them side on.

Stools take up less space than chairs and can be tucked under worktops when not in use. They are a necessity for the housewife who wants to take the weight off her feet as she prepares the vegetables or has her morning cup of coffee. They should be upholstered in washable materials.

Cooking utensils. Most housewives have too many cheap pots and pans. Do not clutter your kitchen unnecessarily. Have fewer, but better, pans. Invest, say, in enamelled cast iron, which looks good, is tough and will go in the oven or on top of the stove.

Two or three really sharp cook's knives will serve you for most food preparation tasks. A wall-mounted can-opener saves time and irritation. Clear glass jars are best for storage. They are cheaper than fancy ones and you can see at a glance just what you are about to run out of! Non-stick ovenware and baking tins look far better than the old-fashioned kind, and save your time, temper and detergent.

Finally, have a fun corner in your kitchen — a portable radio, a shelf on which to read or write, a jug with flowers in season, a pretty poster of a place you have enjoyed on holiday or, depending on age and taste, a photograph of your current pop idol. The kitchen is a large part of a housewife's world, so she should personalise it to her taste and enjoy being in it.

LIGHTING THE KITCHEN

One of the most vital ingredients of kitchen planning is lighting. A good deal of work in the kitchen goes on by artificial light and it is essential that there should be enough of it and that it should be in the right places.

Well designed spotlights help here. They can be fixed at any level and any angle, or fitted into the ceiling at regular intervals.

Another excellent and unobtrusive way to light a kitchen is by setting strip lights under wall cupboards and over the work tops. 'Local' strip lights give a better, softer light than a centre strip light in the ceiling. A light over the cooker is something you would not do without once you have experienced its advantages. Cooker hoods often incorporate one — or you can angle a spotlight over the cooker.

To sum up. The areas which need bright direct light are: the cooker, the sink area, the work tops and the breakfast bar. The one place which demands a hanging light is the dining table.

HEATING AND VENTILATION

The ideal kitchen is warm but not stuffy, with plenty of fresh air and incorporating some method of trapping and dispersing smell and fumes. Given these attributes, that bugbear condensation should be avoided. If you have central heating, a radiator will keep the room warm and air the tea towels. Possibly the central heating boiler itself may be sited in a large kitchen and keep it at an even temperature. Or you may have a country kitchen with a comforting solid fuel cooker. This means that you come down to a lovely warm room in the morning. If you have none of these, then either an infra red wall heater (high on the wall away from children's hands) or an electric blow heater will warm the room quickly.

Ventilation can consist of an extractor fan fitted into one of the window panes and/or a cooker hood built over the cooker, with an extractor fan inside connected to an outside vent. If this is difficult to fit in, you can use a hood which operates with carbon filters and does not need to be vented. The filter has to be changed regularly, but many firms who supply hoods perform this on a contract basis.

If you are building from scratch, it is worth considering fitting glass louvres to one of the kitchen windows. These are adjustable and ventilate the room without letting in a howling draught.

Blinds are ideal in a kitchen. They let in the light, don't get in the way and are so easy to keep clean

LIVING ROOMS
The First Principles

1 The living room is, by definition, for living in. But in your family what does that encompass? Sitting around? Conversing in groups? Watching television? Reading, writing, sewing? The children at their homework? Entertaining neighbours and friends, and the occasional big party? Perhaps your one living area must fulfil all, or many of, these purposes. Perhaps it must double, too, as the family dining room. If so, as a much used room, it must be easy to clean and maintain. It must also be versatile, with seating, lighting and heating arranged so that the room serves individual activity, such as checking the household bills, as well as group activity, such as playing cards.

2 Open-plan, closed plan or a compromise? The choice depends on the size of the family, the size of the room or rooms, the feasibility and cost of structural alterations and, not least, personal taste. A large open-plan area may *seem* chilly and lacking in privacy for the individual even if it is well heated and provided with a suitable periphery for the family loner. There are more ways of dividing a large room than screening off one part entirely; and there are more ways of opening up a small room than removing a communicating wall . . . as the living room designs in this book show.

3 Furnishing and decoration must be apt for a multi-purpose room. Comfortable and informal for the family to relax in. Robust enough to withstand invasion by children. Attractive and welcoming when guests come — for the living room is the showpiece of the house, however much we pretend to scoff at the notion of keeping up with the Joneses.

4 The living room is a sit-down room. Some people prefer an upright chair; others would rather lean back against a soft, resilient support. It is best to have a variety of seating: ample chairs, a sofa for sprawling, stools or pouffes for putting up your feet, cushions that don't disdain the floor. Apart from the main table, indispensable for formally laid meals, small occasional

tables lend mobility. It's irksome to move a chair in front of the television screen only to find there is nothing within reach except the floor on which to rest your coffee cup. Zone the heavier furniture to allow as much 'traffic' space as possible within the room.

5 Scheme colour and pattern in the living room to accord with family tastes, assuming a consensus is possible. The room designs in this book show how flair can transform a room. Bear in mind that people with a true eye for decoration can afford to flout the general rules; most of us cannot. What rules? Very basically that a room scheme is best composed of a main colour (predominating because of the extent of the area to which it is applied rather than because of its brightness or boldness as such), a contrast colour and linking neutral shades.

6 Abundant storage space in wall units or room-dividers frees the body of the living room for its social function and makes the walls work for their existence. Modular units can be added to as the need arises — as it inevitably does, for most families are inveterate magpies.

7 For social purposes, lighting should be soft and atmospheric *around* the room rather than glaring down from a central point, although it is as well to have a ceiling-suspended light over the dining table. For close work: supplementary lights that can be angled to give a direct beam.

8 In any but the mildest climate, adequate background heating is perhaps the principal ingredient of comfort. In addition, an open fire or visibly warming appliance is a psychological as well as physical boost — a cheering focal point on a cold day. Soft wall-to-wall floor covering (and/or rugs) makes for cosiness in the living room. Draughts are flagrantly anti-social and should be stopped at source by proper insulation of doors and windows.

IT LOOKS LIKE AN EXECUTIVE SUITE 1

Smart and shrewdly planned, the living room shown on the previous pages has an executive touch. Flexible units make an 'island' room divider with a pull-out dining table

Everything about the living room pictured on the previous pages spells restrained good taste and an eye for quality and simple good design, although perhaps it is open to question whether the room would stand up to the rough and tumble of family life with youngsters.

The sophisticated colour scheme is white and pale coffee with touches of black, and the backbone of the furnishings is provided by the flexible unit furniture, very cleverly arranged here to do two things — provide ample storage space along one wall, leaving the central part of the room free for chairs and a table and for an unusual room divider. Positioned where it is, the divider leaves comfortable passage space on either side of it, yet it helps to screen the sitting area and, with a television set at just the right height, provides relaxed viewing.

The units in the divider have been fitted together to form a cubic shape. Each of the four sides of the divider offers a variety of storage arrangements. There are adjustable shelves for books and the display of ornaments and other possessions, and there are drawers at the base. Best of all there is a pull-out table. This provides a dining table for four, or it can double as a work table, as a very efficient spotlight is fixed to the shelves above it, giving a strong direct light that serves dining and close work equally well.

Along the window wall the wall units (at the left of the picture on the previous pages) include drawers, shelves and cupboards, one with a pull-down flap on which to stand drinks or even to use as a small desk. The arrangement has maximum flexibility, since the shelves are supported on small pull-out pegs. These can be easily manoeuvred to increase or reduce shelf heights as often as is required.

The ceiling in this room has been lowered so that the units fit flush with it, avoiding a dust trap at the top and giving a much neater finish. Natural pine boards have been used for the ceiling and they look particularly attractive echoing, as they do, the colour of the fitted carpet.

The easy chairs are deep and wide, with squashy cushion for comfort. They are fitted with ball-bearing castors so the can be shifted around easily for watching television or to mak a cosier group for conversation. The four folding black chair at the pull-out table against the room divider can be stacke out of sight when not in use.

Pattern in this living room is confined to the curtain. Because they pick up the two colours used consistently in the other furnishings — white and coffee — it has been pos sible to use a strong geometric design without this provin overpowering.

An uncluttered, highly efficient room of this kind — it cou well be an executive suite in an office — does need a gentl pretty touch here and there if it is to spell out home. It come in the masses of white chrysanthemums, informally arrange in a plain glass vase on the coffee table.

Unit furniture of the standard shown is far from cheap but it is a good investment because of its flexibility. It cor fers all the advantages of built-in furniture without the dis advantages. As well as being flexible enough to be rearrange in a different way to fit a revamped room, or perhaps different way of living, it can — unlike built-ins — be dismantle and taken with you if you are moving house.

Dividing an open-plan room with an 'island' fitment i ideal if the room is not too large, as it gives a degree o privacy in the centre near the seating area, without wastin too much floor space. If a greater degree of screening ha been felt to be desirable, similar units could have been use side by side to meet one of the walls in the room, leaving jus one opening as a passage way.

Whatever the permutations you decide upon for your pa ticular needs and tastes, the main plus factor *is* the pe mutability of this type of fitment. You can start modestl perhaps with a block of four drawers, one cupboard and tw or three shelves, and add to the combination little by little.

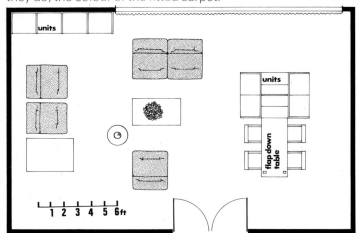

Careful positioning of 'island' unit cuts off sitting area

Elizabeth Whiting

COLOUR SCHEME THAT IS BASED ON THE CARPET 2

COLOUR SCHEME THAT IS BASED ON THE CARPET 2

The first floor of an old house was re-designed to produce a highly individual and modern open-plan living room, with a green and gold striped carpet setting the colour scheme

You would never guess that the strikingly modern interior pictured here and on the previous page belongs to a 19th-century terraced house. The architect in charge of the conversion re-designed the whole of the first floor, removing the wall between the front and back rooms to make an open-plan living room with an interesting shape.

Two steps lead up to the dining area, lined on two sides with shelves, cupboards and filing drawers, so that it can easily double as a study during the day and everything can be stored out of sight at meal times. The ceiling in this area was lowered and a single spotlight inset to shine directly over the dining table.

The highly original green and gold striped carpet was designed by the architect and specially woven for him by a carpet firm. The design matches ceramic tiles which are used to form a hearth for the open fireplace and as a floor for the balcony on to which the living room opens. The same carpet is used in the hall and on the staircase, giving the whole house a unified appearance.

In the living area the large and comfortable settee has down-filled cushions, covered in wool fabric, and the settee base is covered with carpet, a most unusual touch but one which works very well.

Note how the cushions pick up the gold colour of the carpet. The chair with a foot rest is also on a carpet-covered base and can become a day bed with the addition of the foot rest.

The architect turned the window in the living room into French windows to open on to the balcony. A natural-coloured blind is used instead of curtains and the windows are lined on both sides with bookshelves. The uprights of the bookshelves are painted white and the actual shelves covered in green felt in keeping with the green and gold colour scheme of the whole room.

The walls and ceiling are white, and white louvred doors lead into the hall. Light is provided by spotlights in the ceiling and there is a very striking coffee table made of stainless steel.

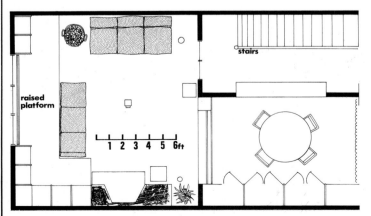

Plan shows dining, sitting areas in relation to each other

A FABULOUS ROOM

The materials are tough, the storage units can be added to and the seating is comfortable. Best of all, everything can be switched about to suit the mood of the moment

Here is a near-perfect example of a living room that young members of the family would happily call their own. And, when allowed in, their elders would find it tolerable.

The room is youthfully cheerful. More to the point, it is easy to keep clean and everything in it is movable. The hard-wearing rush matting is not fitted but loose-laid, so that it can come up to leave a smooth floor for informal dancing. The plump cushions, which provide comfortable seating, are covered in tough cotton, the white and navy stripes giving the room a perkily nautical air. And the back cushions can be used on the floor to provide additional seats when there's a crowd being entertained.

The low storage units at the right of the picture are designed to hold a record player and records comfortably, and the corner linking these with the seats is filled neatly with two fitments in the role of a coffee table with storage room inside. There is a gap left for stacking things against the wall — rolls of paper, posters designed for later display or whatever. A low ceiling light gives spot illumination for reading or writing in the corner.

Not only is the seating arrangement inexpensive, but it has the advantage of leaving plenty of space in the room for a working table — an essential item for students — that could double as a dining table, leaving the youngsters free to entertain their own friends while their parents use the family dining room or the kitchen (if there is nowhere else to which discreetly to retreat).

The kind of space-saving room scheme shown could also be deployed successfully as the sitting end of a bed sitting-room, as it would leave space at the other end of the room for a bed and possibly a flap table which could be folded out of the way when not in use. The storage units at the right of the picture could be supplemented, or could link with a plain white wardrobe if the room was also used as a bedroom. A mirror on the top of one of the units would provide a simple dressing table if the room belonged to a girl.

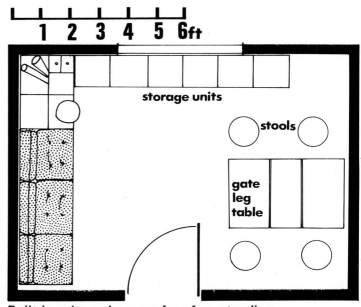

Built-in units make room for a free-standing table and stools

Good design transcends age barriers. That is one lesson taught by the tasteful blending of modern and traditional in this elegant room. Another is that what looks luxurious can be achieved quite economically

Modulated colour can exert as much influence on the total looks of a room as bold colouring, and it makes for a restful and relaxing atmosphere — as the living room pictured here demonstrates.

In this high-ceilinged capacious period room, the all-white scheme is broken only by the handsome black and white checked sofa and by the blue green mounts of the drawings, hung at eye level on the right hand wall.

Here is a room that breathes luxury, from the sweep of silk floor-length curtains, hung on a brass pole running the length of the wall, to the cream fur rugs on the veined vinyl floor.

The centrepiece is the large glass table on a stainless steel frame. The table is large enough to hold drinks, without need to dislodge the magazines or books normally scattered on it. It could even cope with informal fork suppers for visiting friends.

The white-covered sectional settee not only provides ample seating but has the effect of creating an intimate conversation area through the use of a corner seat which links the two settees at right angles to each other.

A handsome silver candelabra and cut glass decanters on a silver galleried tray are gracious touches which recall the room's ancestry (18th century) and prove that good design knows no age barriers. See how well they go with the really modern glass table.

A room like this need not be as much of a luxury as it looks at first sight. The white settee could be covered in wipe-clean upholstery. The curtains and the cushions could be made in easy-care fabrics which are machine washable and need only minimum ironing. The vinyl floor needs only a damp mop to keep it clean, and the fur rugs could be replaced with a pair in man-made fabrics which wash easily.

In fact, today's fabrics and finishes on the one hand and, on the other, automatic washing machines which have different programmes to cope with most materials mean that white and pastel colours can be used freely throughout the house, giving the home decorator far more scope.

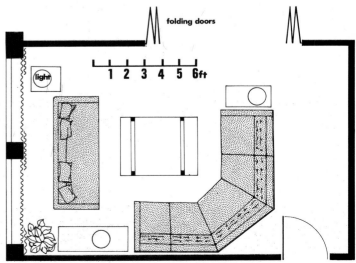

folding doors

1 2 3 4 5 6ft

light

Grouping settees provides intimate conversation area

A ROOM RICH IN PERMUTATIONS 5

Furniture and fitments in the room seen on the previous pages compose a conversation enclave with a study area beyond it. But their mobility offers a choice of other layouts

The feature that immediately catches the eye in the living-room pictured on the two previous pages is the high cylindrical shelf fitment. It's an original component in the division of the room into a snug conversation area in the foreground and the study area beyond. Yet, because the room is compartmentalised by means of furniture arrangement rather than by a bulky divider or arbitrary screen, the open-plan is truly open and fluid, and it allows of simple re-arrangement of the components to suit quite different needs.

What helps towards the versatility of the room is that practically all the furniture and fitments are mobile. This goes even for the cylindrical shelf fitment. In the arrangement shown it acts as a visual divider between the sitting and study ends of the living room. But it could be pushed against the wall to leave more space for general family activity or for entertaining guests.

In the sitting enclave, six chairs face one another across the flowered rug, which provides the only pattern in the room. They are designed almost as though they were car seats. They have no legs and no arms but, for comfort, have gently sloping backs.

The three-sided enclosure of the sitting area is completed by two low fitments in line under the windows. Loose cushions on them provide extra seating – so that eight or more people could engage in animated conversation within a small square and, noise level permitting, an uninvolved member of the family could still read or write at the desk only a few feet beyond. With the cushions removed, the low fitments could alternatively become table tops. Their shallow bottom shelves hold books and magazines.

The six chairs and the twin fitments are on castors, so that, including the cylindrical display and storage fitment, all the components of the sitting area are fully mobile and can be moved to facilitate wholesale rearrangement of the room.

Rearrangement apart, lightweight mobile furniture like th[is] helps greatly to ease the housewife's chores. If the furnitur[e] can be moved around easily, thorough vacuuming of du[st] traps becomes a far less ponderous exercise.

It is interesting to see how the wide gold band which run[s] round the top of the room has the effect both of lowering th[e] ceiling and echoing the colour scheme with its gold carpe[t] and upholstery. The gold band provides, too, a neat alternativ[e] to a pelmet, hiding the curtain track.

The layout of the room would lend itself equally well to [a] living room with a dining end. A table and chairs could b[e] fitted in the area which now houses the desk, and the lo[w] white dividing shelf on the study side could have doors fitte[d] on what would then be the dining side to act as a sideboar[d]. The top, covered with a plastic laminate, would make a usef[ul] extra surface on which to stand the serving dishes, and som[e]where for the man of the house to do the carving (if indeed h[e] does it!). Too often the dining end of a living room suffers fro[m] lack of space. Any housewife who has tried to serve a thre[e] course meal to six people with nowhere to put plates or dishe[s] will know what a disadvantage this can be. A trolley is on[e] answer, but only a fairly large one is much use.

Finally there is no reason why the layout shown coul[d] not be adapted to bed-sitting-room living. A divan coul[d] take the place of one set of sectional seats. The desk coul[d] then be used for dining when the owner was alone and, f[or] entertaining guests, a folding card table with a pretty tabl[e] cloth and four stacking chairs could be fitted in the spac[e] behind the cylindrical shelf fitment. Built-in cupboards cou[ld] be installed along the wall facing the windows. The result: [a] neat, attractive living arrangement for bachelors of either sex[.]

There would be an added bonus in the fact that the smal[l] scale, highly adaptable furniture could be put to differen[t] uses if and when the owner moved to a larger flat or house.

1 2 3 4 5 6ft

swivel unit

seats

seats

storage unit

Plan of room (picture on previous page) arranged for work and play

CUSTOM-BUILT WALL FITMENT SETS THE SCENE 6

CUSTOM-BUILT WALL FITMENT SETS THE SCENE 6

Taking up the whole of one side, a made-to-measure set of shelves and cupboards provides the dramatic focal point (see previous page) in this brown-walled living room

You can build shelves in many ways and at varying cost, from the very basic plank of wood supported on two battens in an alcove to the sort of specially designed and made-to-measure fitment featured in the picture on the previous page. For the latter you need the imagination and skill to design something that is in keeping with the room scheme and that will meet your storage needs. And, unless you pride yourself as an expert craftsman, you need a good professional carpenter to carry out the work for you.

The particular fitment in the living room shown is designed to take up the whole of one wall in the room and fits neatly under the cornice at the top of the wall. The base is made up of a series of cupboards with twin doors, picked out with moulding and handsome brass handles. The tops of these cupboards are used for displaying ornaments and other objects, and the shelves are fitted above them. A decorative feature of this wall fitment is provided by the curved wooden tops which give an elegant finish to the whole assembly. This curve can be copied quite easily to give even the most rudimentary home-made shelves a less utilitarian look.

Painted white, the shelf fitment in the room shown stands out dramatically against the rest of the walls, which are covered with brown hessian, and the thick carpet that matches the hessian. Hessian is a good way to cover living room walls, as the texture is as attractive as the very wide range of colours it comes in. But it is not cheap and considerable care is needed in putting it up. However, hessian makes a superb background for hanging pictures and even one wall covered with it can look very good, provided the rest of the room either contrasts with it or blends in subtly.

The pretty living room in the pictures is furnished with a mixture of modern and Victorian furniture, both of which look their best against the dark brown walls. Dark walls can serve a living room very faithfully. They will not make it seem at all gloomy, provided there is plenty of white paintwork to set them off. They can enrich the effect of pictures hung on them, and make flower arrangements stand out like a Dutch painting.

But dark coloured walls do demand careful selection of accessory colours; subtly distributed, softer shades provide a welcome counterfoil. Note, for instance, how the pink cushions on the pretty cane chair in the picture on this page give a lift to the whole room.

On the previous page is shown another corner of this living room, with a built-in fitment housing books and ornaments. In contrast to the crowded, busy feeling of that fitment, this corner has been kept simple. It provides a quiet oasis for anyone wishing to write a letter at the bureau or to read in the comfy armchair in the corner. The table lamp on the bureau gives spot lighting for reading or working. The dark colour of the wall makes the one large painting stand out in sharp relief

A ROOMFUL OF DRAMATIC IDEAS 7

A ROOMFUL OF DRAMATIC IDEAS 7

Golden decorative discs on the walls; unusual use of red blinds; chunky divan seating. It's a room expressing confident flair

The dramatic looking room shown here and on the previous pages has several out-of-the-ordinary but adaptable ideas.

Echoing the shape of the back rests, the decorative golden discs on the walls give the living room a space-age look. They could be copied by covering hardboard or even cardboard with gold foil or tinsel paper — to make an inexpensive substitute for paintings, assuming that their uncompromising boldness is to your taste.

Another unusual note is the use of the blinds, which also pick up the disc theme in a fabric with crimson discs on a lighter red. One of the blinds is used flat on the end wall in the manner of a tapestry. The other blind can be lowered to partition off the desk at the far end of the room.

In fact the whole furnishing concept of this living room is somewhat unconventional. The five plush divans, in their scarlet fitted covers with semi-circular cushions forming the back rests, seem to invite audience participation in a drama that is about to be enacted. They help to divide the sitting area from the 'study' at one end and the dining area in the corner. Scarlet predominates in the room against a background of white in the walls and the fluffy carpet with its matching rugs. Accent touches of forest green are used for

Elizabeth Whiting

a cushion, one divan base and — another unusual note — on the radiator along the wall at the study end (see the picture on the previous page).

A built-in shelf fitment, with books on the shelves at its base, partly divides the room from the front door and the 'study' end. The room makes an immediate impact on visitors as they enter through the front door, for the intervening lobby is minimal; but the lobby area does have a thick rug to counter muddy shoes. A round table lacquered in red stands in the centre of the sitting area and there is space for a dining table and white pedestal chairs.

Futuristic and opulent as the room may appear, it has the practical asset of versatility. It could be turned into a double bed-sitter. The seating area could be re-positioned easily. And there are actually enough divans to make comfortable beds for five people!

Plan showing allocation for work; relaxing; dining

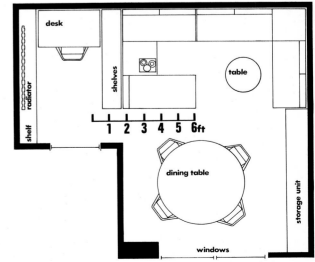

desk

radiator

shelf

shelves

table

1 2 3 4 5 6ft

dining table

storage unit

windows

ALERT TO GARDEN, BLIND TO ROAD 8

When, in the morning, the curtains are drawn back there's a garden view through a glass wall. The opposite wall blanks out road and traffic

The open-plan living room pictured on the previous two pages embodies a useful option for homemakers with some reservations on open-plan living: sliding doors can shut off the dining room at the right of the picture.

This is a thoughtfully planned as well as a welcoming room. The right-hand wall, facing the road, has only small clerestory windows let in at intervals. This affords privacy for the owners from the public gaze and reduces traffic noise, a major consideration these days in any built-up area. In contrast, the opposite wall is entirely glass, offering abundant natural light and a total view of the garden and swimming pool outside. The creamy, semi-sheer curtains on the left can be drawn right across it, giving a unified look with the white brick of the other walls.

A simple hole-in-the-wall fireplace has been inserted over a raised hearth. The level makes it possible to tend the fireplace without bending unduly and there is the bonus of spare shelf space. Quarry tiles are used near the hearth and at the end of the room opening on to the garden. They are a practical, easy-to-clean flooring in areas bearing heavy domestic traffic.

A noteworthy feature of the furnishing in this living room is the long, low shelf-cum-bench that runs along the whole of one wall. It is a significant space-saver, accommodating a record player, tape recorder and speaker, books and flowers, and with the aid of cushions also provides extra seating. A slotted shelf/bench fitment of this kind comes well within do-it-yourself capacity.

One of the charms of this room is the lack of clutter. The low furniture is on the right scale for the proportions of the room. The well designed three-seater sofa has simple, fluent lines. It's a piece of furniture that an experienced craftsman could make himself by following the instructions given on these pages. Facing the linked chairs and interposed coffee table, it intimately defines the conversation area.

Textures and colours have been used discriminately. The ceiling and the floor are in warm wood; three of the walls are plain white brick. All the furniture is in pale wood. The upholstery and the rug are in plain caramel tones. Only the coral and peacock of the scatter cushions introduce a brighter note, echoed in the bold modern painting.

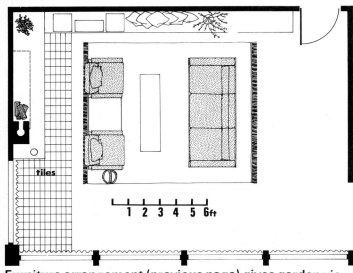

Furniture arrangement (previous page) gives garden view

The finished sofa

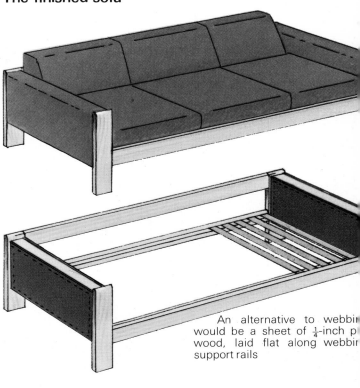

An alternative to webbing would be a sheet of ¼-inch ply wood, laid flat along webbing support rails

DESIGN FOR A THREE-SEATER SOFA

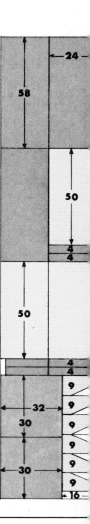

Wood should be beech, and must be planed all round. Sizes given here refer to unplaned wood. You will need: three lengths of 4 x 1¼ x 78-inch timber for back and front rails; four of 4 x 1¼ x 24-inch for legs; two of 2 x 2 x 72-inch for rails to support webbing; four of 3 x 1¼ x 28⅞-inch for top and bottom of arm frames; four of 3 x 1¼ x 12¾-inch for sides of arm frames. In hardboard, you will need the following: four bits of standard ⅛ cut 28⅞ x 15 inches for box sides of arms; four of hardboard, cut 28¾ x 15 for extra sides to upholster; two strips of hardboard 28¾ x 3 for undersides of arm pads. To make seat cushions, use firm grade foam: three pieces 4 inches thick x 21 deep x 24 wide. Use medium grade foam for back cushions: three slabs 15 inches deep by 24 wide of 4-inch foam; plus three wedges cut to taper from 4 inches to nothing to form sloping back. To cover full face and top of cushions, use one-inch foam, cut to fit; two strips of one-inch foam to fit tops of arms, cut 24 x 4 inches; 6⅔ yards of 50-inch upholstery fabric, cut according to diagram (right). Cutting guide at right. Green represents seats; yellow, backs; blue, arms.

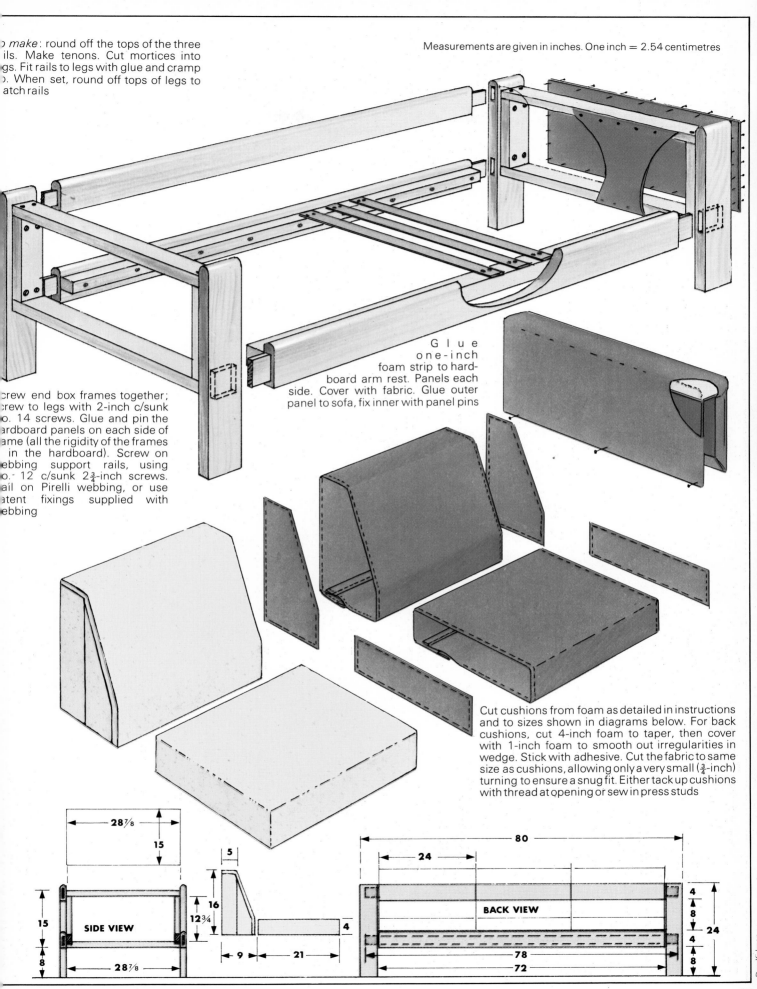

o make: round off the tops of the three ils. Make tenons. Cut mortices into gs. Fit rails to legs with glue and cramp . When set, round off tops of legs to atch rails

crew end box frames together; crew to legs with 2-inch c/sunk o. 14 screws. Glue and pin the ardboard panels on each side of ame (all the rigidity of the frames in the hardboard). Screw on ebbing support rails, using o. 12 c/sunk 2¾-inch screws. ail on Pirelli webbing, or use atent fixings supplied with ebbing

Glue one-inch foam strip to hard-board arm rest. Panels each side. Cover with fabric. Glue outer panel to sofa, fix inner with panel pins

Cut cushions from foam as detailed in instructions and to sizes shown in diagrams below. For back cushions, cut 4-inch foam to taper, then cover with 1-inch foam to smooth out irregularities in wedge. Stick with adhesive. Cut the fabric to same size as cushions, allowing only a very small (¾-inch) turning to ensure a snug fit. Either tack up cushions with thread at opening or sew in press studs

28⅞   15

SIDE VIEW

15   12¾   16   15   8

28⅞

5   16   4

9   21

BACK VIEW

80   24   78   72

4   8   24   4   8

A ROOM FURNISHED WITH BOOKS 9

he floor-to-ceiling bookshelves give a reposeful, scholarly character to this graceful room
ith its antique furniture and soft colours

This room is part of a 19th century addition to a country house that was built 200 years earlier. The owners have furnished it with some choice pieces of family furniture. The room is lined by hundreds of books which demonstrate how handsomely books can decorate a room, even if on a much humbler scale than this. The room serves partly as a library and study, partly as a family sitting room.

The bookshelves, which were designed by the owner of the house, are in keeping with the beautiful proportions of the room and complement the lace work cornice which edges the ceiling. The uprights of the bookshelves are topped with a decorative motif, and the tops and bases of the shelf units are moulded as befits the period atmosphere.

The bay window is 4 ft. (1.21 m.) deep. It has proved to be the ideal place for the handsome kneehole desk. During the day, the light pours in all round it; at night, when the lovely old rose curtains are drawn, a table lamp casts a soft glow.

A Persian rug lies in front of the Victorian marble fireplace and a deep armchair covered in a rich French velvet offers comfort by the fire. The only bright colour in this mellow room is provided by the yellow fitted carpet, which is a perfect foil to the browns and dark reds.

Worth noting: no ceiling lights disturb the gentleness of this room; instead, table lamps with parchment-coloured shades cast a ruminative glow at night and pick out the sheen of leather-bound books, the soft colours of flowers in a bowl and the collection of ornaments lovingly gathered over the years.

Certainly the owners of this room are fortunate in possessing graceful furniture, priceless accessories, and beautifully bound volumes. But the room has lessons for most home-planners. One of these is that floor-to-ceiling bookshelves dress up a room and instantly seem to make it home. They need not be filled only with books. The books — and they could be paperbacks instead of first editions — can be interspersed with ornaments.

Another lesson to be learned from this study that doubles as a family room is the gentle and muted colour scheme forming an appropriate background for leisure and relaxation.

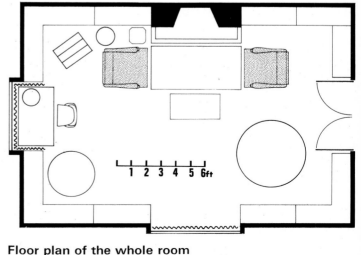

Floor plan of the whole room

THE DIVIDER THAT COMMUNICATES 10

It is difficult to believe that this spacious-looking living room with a lovely view of trees and grass and a discreetly screened dining room is actually in quite a small modern flat.

The dining end of the room, seen through the screen in the first picture, has its own source of light in a large window. The screen is an unusual divider made of patterned brick, painted white. The decorative pattern has the effect of successfully screening the dining table and the chairs, while letting in plenty of light from each end of the room.

The cleverly designed wooden fitment, which appears to be a continuation of the screen, is open-framed to about 1 ft. (304.8 mm.) of the floor to sustain the open-work feeling of the screen. It houses a cocktail cabinet in the base, with doors on both sides of the room, and the hi-fi equipment, with a lighting unit built in above it, while the top makes a very useful wine rack. There's enough room

left beyond the divider to form a good passageway to the door (at the left of the first picture), which leads into the rest of the flat. And a hatch at a convenient height leads into the kitchen from the dining end.

Another unusual feature in this room is the built-in fitment above the settee in the sitting area (at left of the first picture). This holds the speakers for the hi-fi system and provides shelves for display. Above the fitment, fluorescent tubes are hidden behind frosted glass doors, enlivened with a stylised design in orange and pink to pick out the main colour scheme in the room.

The colourful curtains in a harlequin pattern of pinks, oranges, yellows and brown (second picture) are lit up by fluorescent tubes hidden behind a pelmet which runs across the whole window wall, a little below the ceiling.

A strikingly incisive stainless steel chimney is fixed above

It both partitions and unifies the dining and sitting areas. And, in line with it, a fitment astutely houses a cocktail cabinet, hi-fi and a wine rack at the top

a shelf to form a mock fireplace. The shelf, covered with plastic laminate, holds logs, a small portable television set and various ornaments.

The deep and comfortable settee and matching armchairs are covered in a beige and white checked fabric. The carpet is lilac pink and over it is laid a long haired rug in the same colours as the curtains.

This is a room that emphatically expresses its owners' taste, imagination and ideas, reflected particularly in the singular screening device.

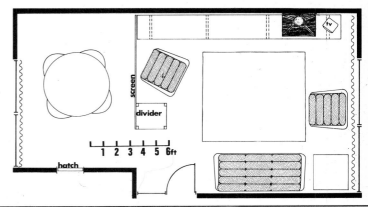

Open-work screen partially separates one third of total area — the dining from the sitting part

The built-in wall seats give intimacy to this snugly designed corner, partitioned off from the main part of the living room by the fireplace wall on the right of the picture

The owners of this warm-looking room wanted a 'snuggery' that would provide an area of privacy within their open-plan living room. So at the design stage they decided to partition off a corner of the living room by means of a half wall, which would incorporate a farmhouse-style open fireplace.

The comfortable 'snuggery' is brick-built and painted white, like the rest of the walls, and comfortable foam rubber cushions cover the seating. Bright cushions in red and green provide a back rest and a touch of colour in an otherwise brown and white room.

A brick breast, topped with quarry tiles (at left background in the picture), provides solid shelving and (in the foreground) bricks with a wooden top enclose the seating from the rest of the room. Warm quarry tiles cover the floor — warm in look and feel, as the house has underfloor heating.

The wooden ceiling carries exposed structural timbers and glass spheres between the beams give dramatic lighting to the 'snuggery'. Wood is used, too, for the two long book-shelves on the left of the picture.

The texture is one of the charms here: the rough texture of the bricks, the knotty wood and the knubbly weave of the oatmeal-coloured rug.

While the area shown is only part of the living room in this house, it is interesting to note how space-saving the L-shaped built-in seating is, and how effectively it could be adapted to a really small living room. If built-in seating is out of the question, two settees at right angles to each other, with a square coffee table to fill the gap between them, would provide maximum seating in a minimum floor area. An additional low coffee table, drawn up within arm's reach of the settees, would complete a corner for conversation and drinks.

In a large open-plan area, the idea of a living room within a living room is worth adopting. Where the family is numerous and of all ages and tastes, friction can be avoided if individuals can retire to the subsidiary room to write or read in privacy. Alternatively, the 'snuggery' could be turned into a television-viewing room.

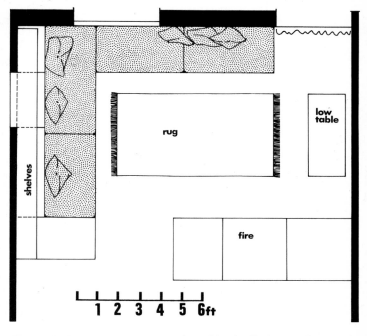

Floor plan shows the space freed by built-in seating

EVERY INCH HERE IS A SPACE-SAVER 12

The living area pictured on the two previous pages is little more than a large alcove with a window, but the wall fitments free enough space for a foursome to sit around comfortably

Plenty of cupboard space and open shelves for books and ornaments, a shelf for the radio and a pull-down desk are provided by the handsomely designed unit fitments in the living room pictured on the two previous pages.

The units occupy two walls from floor to ceiling, giving unbroken lines and avoiding dust traps at the top. Surfaced in white, they blend beautifully with the rest of an emphatically white room, the large and comfortable chairs also being white in a spongeable finish. Two armless chairs are placed side by side to form a sofa, and an armchair faces them across the room from a low table with a plastic laminate top on a stainless steel base. Another low table at the side of the armchair is useful for drinks and magazines. The sleek chair pictured drawn up to the desk can be pressed into general service, so that this small area has ample capacity for four people to engage in close conversation.

Colour in a white room comes from the warm orange carpet and the modern lithograph in orange tones which hangs in a rather unusual eye-catching manner in front of the net curtains. Although it may interfere with the view through the window, this idea has something to commend it if there is no wall space available for pictures and provided the picture so suspended has a light frame.

Well made, elegantly finished unit fitments are not inexpensive to buy. On the other hand, they can be bought and assembled stage by stage. Indeed, a living room can be planned rather like a kitchen, adding more as and when the family budget allows it.

The room pictured on the previous pages could be turned into a bed-sitting-room if a pull-down bed were to be fitted into the tall cupboard fitment in the centre of the right-hand wall. At night the chairs could be pushed out of the way and one of the coffee tables would become a bedside table. In the morning the bed would just fold back behind the cupboard doors and the room would take on its living room role.

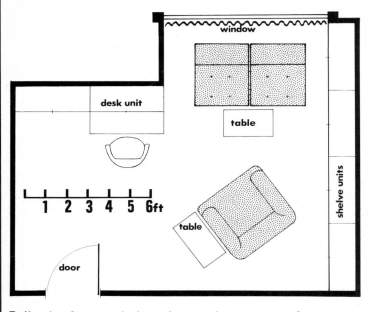

Full value from a window alcove; picture on previous pages

WOOD IN

WOOD IN A MAJOR ROLE 13

A pine ceiling, a glowing teak wood floor and a simply designed room-divider in natural wood are principal constituents of a spruce and practical room

The warm tones of different woods and white create a simple yet distinctive background in the living room (previous pages) in an architect's home.

Parana pine is used for the ceiling and for the frames of the purpose-built windows, designed with one door opening on to a patio, facing full south, and with side openings to two of the windows. The result is, in effect, a glass wall through which the light pours, the slats of the white venetian blind exerting control.

The curtains are noteworthy. They are made of plain, undyed theatrical backdrop material in a thick knobbly texture in cream. This is an inexpensive way to curtain a very large area from floor to ceiling, and the drapes are in keeping with the colours and textures in the room.

The room-divider (at the right of the picture on the previous page) separating the dining area is one of the main features of the room. Made of parana pine, it is very simple in design, but provides plenty of shelf space, accessible from each side of the room, and screens the sitting area without robbing the rest of the room of any light. It provides a home for books and magazines, and displays ornaments. A casual touch is the unframed print which has been pinned on with thumb tacks along the edge of one shelf. Instructions for making a similar kind of simple divider are given, with diagrams, on these pages.

A simple hole-in-the-wall open fireplace has a hearth built of blue engineering bricks which are heat-resistant; the surround is in steel and a narrow brass hood fits sleekly into the top.

The floor surface comprises teak wood blocks. A plain white rug covers the conversation and television-viewing sector, while a small orange mat is superimposed facing the hearth.

DESIGN FOR A ROOM-DIVIDER

A sturdy set of timber storage units to construct at home. Here is how

The dimensions of the framework must be worked out according to the measurements of your room. The uprights and shelves should be made from 12 x $1\frac{1}{4}$-inch timber. You will also need sufficient aluminium angle cut into 10-inch lengths to support each shelf at both ends; and a quantity of screws.

To make Cut the shelves to 30 inches long, and the uprights to the correct height to suit your room. Sandpaper and polish the timber. Cut 10-inch lengths of aluminium angle for shelves. Drill three holes in one side of each length and two holes in the other. Countersink. Fix angles to the uprights using $\frac{1}{2}$-inch no. 8 screws in the appropriate positions to support the shelves. Now assemble the whole framework. If the height of the divider is to be lower than the ceiling, this operation can take place on the floor. Set out the uprights on the floor (one end flush to the wall, the other firmly wedged), with the shelves laid in between. Lay tie rails across the top side of the structure. Mark off and drill screw holes. Secure rails to uprights with screws. Turn over the whole framework to attach tie rails on the other side in the same way. Stand unit upright. Attach one end of the structure firmly to the wall with wood blocks set at shoulder height. Finally, fix the whole to the floor with a strong bracket.

If the divider is to touch the ceiling, you will have to assemble it upright. This is slightly more difficult and needs another pair of hands to help. First, attach one upright to the wall (with wood blocks as described above). Next, with an extra person holding the second upright in position, lay on the first lot of shelves. Hold up a length of tie rail. Mark and drill screw holes. Fix on rail with screws. Repeat with another length of tie rail on the other side of the structure. Repeat the whole operation with the third upright; then with the fourth, and so on until all the uprights are secured in position. Now attach the remainder of tie rails. Finally, fix the structure to the floor with a strong bracket.

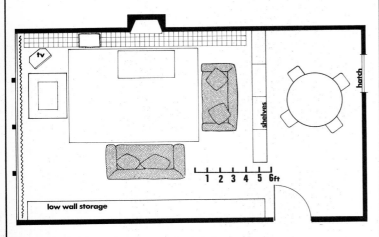

Floor plan of living room pictured on previous page

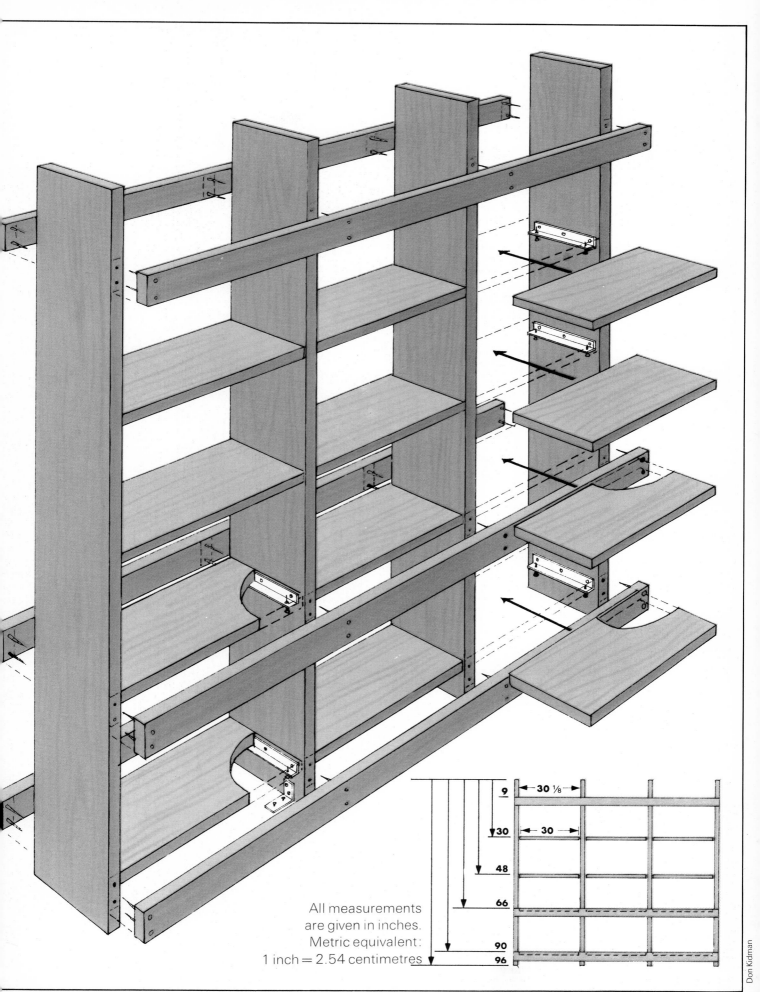

All measurements
are given in inches.
Metric equivalent:
1 inch = 2.54 centimetres

30 1/8
9
30
30
48
66
90
96

Deck chairs, painted whitewood shelves and a medley of cushions in bright stripes and checks give this living room the jaunty atmosphere of a holiday home

The deckchairs and the informality seem to stamp this pretty and colourful room as the heart of a simple holiday home — with the beach or landing-stage not far away. Equally it could serve as an occasional ante-room in a family house anywhere.

The room was equipped and furnished on a shoestring, but there's nothing gimcrack about it.

Three sets of whitewood shelves are placed side by side under the window and painted white and scarlet. The long settee comprises a thin foam rubber mattress on a wooden base, which is then covered with a profusion of cushions in orange and white — plain, checked and striped in a gay medley. Remove the cushions, and you have a comfortable spare bed for a friend staying overnight. The simple wooden coffee table is large enough to offer sit-down snack meals for four people. There is a deep white shelf built in above the sofa to carry books and magazines and to hold the adjustable reading lamp.

The rest of the lighting comes from a decorative pair of orange and white ceramic shades hanging very low over the coffee table. An old-fashioned phonograph and a modern stereo record player sit happily side by side on the shelves. Old prints hang on the wall, and a fun butterfly in scarlet paper is pinned to the striped blue curtains. A Mediterranean-blue fitted carpet adds to the holiday look.

Almost stealing the scene in this living room are the two blue-painted deckchairs. There's much to be said for deck-chairs in any free-and-easy living room, though clearly they would be out of place in an opulent setting. Deck chairs can double for garden use and as extra seating indoors. They are lightweight, fold up and can be stacked flat. They accommodate virtually every sitting or reclining posture. Backrests and cushions are no problem. And deckchair fabric is available in a wide choice of plain colours and patterns.

The room shown here could well make a cheap yet comfortable living room in the first home of a young couple. Nothing in it need be discarded when they can afford more urbane furnishings — whether the deckchairs (for the garden) or the shelves (for the children's room).

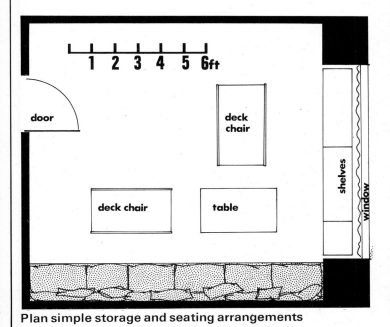

Plan simple storage and seating arrangements

WITH BEACH LOOK

Easy to keep clean and maintain, this all-wood room makes a cheerful bed-sitter in a holiday home. It would suit a loft conversion or a simple home extension

The walls and the ceiling in this warm and cheerful room are in sealed wood, which means that all they require to keep them clean is a wipe with a damp sponge and they need never be decorated — a very important point in a youngsters' room or in a holiday house where both labour and expense have to be kept to the minimum.

A tough cord carpet in a rich golden brown goes well with the wood and makes a practical floor covering. The furniture is hard-wearing and simple in the extreme. Two divans set end to end form a long and comfortable sofa for lounging, and become two beds at night. The wooden bases have drawers for storage and foam rubber mattresses in tough cotton covers with matching back cushions provide comfortable seating. A medley of scatter cushions make for extra comfort.

The other side of the room (foreground of picture) houses a large pine dining table. The dining or lounging chairs are slightly more sophisticated versions of ordinary canvas garden chairs. They have padded seat cushions. Two striking bright orange tables on castors provide occasional tables with storage room in the base.

Light comes from a low ceiling light hanging over the dining table and a row of three scarlet adjustable lamps fitted on to a narrow shelf, built above the sofa, which holds books, a painting, ornaments and a storm lantern — useful out of doors on dark nights in the countryside.

The furnishing scheme of the room would lend itself to a living room exclusive to teenage members of a family. Such a room could result from converting the loft or by adding on a simple extension. In the latter case the wood on the wall would act as insulation, making the room much warmer as well as providing an attractive and long lasting wall finish.

The two divans placed end to end in the room that is shown are a good way of providing a long stretch of seating where the shape of the room suits such an arrangement. The end-to-end positioning leaves more space in the centre of a room — perhaps for a dining table and chairs.

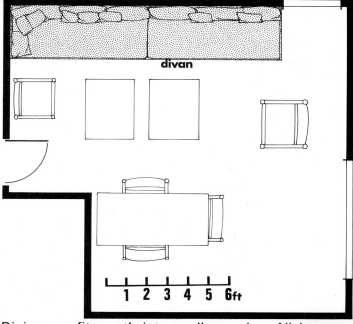

divan

1 2 3 4 5 6ft

Dining area fits neatly into smaller section of living room

This living room is furnished without clutter to lie nicely low, giving the illusion of being a larger room than it actually is

Of its unpretentious kind, this is an impeccable room. The furniture is grouped to save space. The small, low chests, and the low-hanging pictures contrive between them to keep the whole 'operational' level of the room low and therefore make it seem far loftier and more spacious than it in fact is.

The settees are joined to form an L-shape, making good use of a corner of the room and providing, too, a wholly satisfactory niche for conversation. Covered in an off-white fabric, they seem to merge into the wall, whereas obtrusive colours would have had the effect of crowding the room.

The low, light wood chests, designed like campaign chests, look neater than furniture on legs would in this setting. They also provide plenty of storage space and table top surfaces at exactly the right height. The pictures are hung just above the chests, and the low pendant lights fulfil their role of concentrating spot lighting where it is wanted.

On its brass base, the long, low marble-topped coffee table introduces a luxury look to an essentially practical scheme of decoration. It could be moved nearer to the settees and is the right size to go with them.

The warm orange rug, the scatter cushions and the yellow light pendants bring a note of brightness to what is otherwise in effect a monochrome room — but neither a dull one nor a cold-looking one. Neutral colours as seen here form a very good basis for living room colour schemes. They are undistracting and easier to live with than strident colours. Neutrals are a safe background, too, for pictures, books and ornaments which add colour in various measure to any room.

In so small a room as this, it is just as important to avoid warring textures as to avoid warring or obtrusive colours. Silks and velvets call for fitted carpets and smooth paper or paint on the wall, and the warm sheen of mahogany or rosewood furniture. Rougher textured and more informal fabrics, like wool tweed or thick cotton, go well with a wood floor, a cord carpet, fur rugs; perhaps whitewashed brick walls or a textured wallpaper, or even pine panelling on one or more walls.

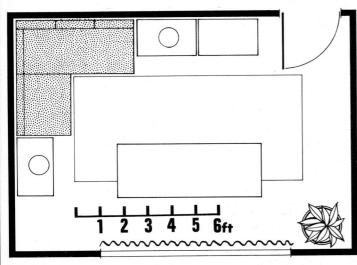

Floor plan with positions of doors and windows

A STREAMLINED FAMILY ROOM 17

A complete storage wall made up of units leaves the remainder of the room free both for restless children and concentrating parents

Size alone does not add up to a family room, in which ideally parents and children should be able to follow their separate pursuits at ease without getting on one another's nerves.

The factors that do make for a good family room (and harmony) are exemplified here.

It is modern in style but relaxing and unclinical. There's

enough floor place for scampering youngsters. A contributing factor here is the storage space along the whole of one wall. This storage wall takes shelves, cupboards, a pull-down desk and, among other things, the television set that reposes, when not in use, behind the white doors in the centre of the unit.

The burnt-orange carpet is the right medium shade not to show tell-tale marks and makes a warm surface for the children at their games to sprawl on. For their off-the-floor games there are three sturdy, square coffee tables with a plastic finish that is proof against knocks and spills and that will take hot plates. The large deep chairs in brown covers on the simplest of white frames are likewise robust — tough enough to withstand children's kicking shoes. Father's chair is about the only luxurious piece of furniture. But it's practical: the black upholstery is spongeable.

It is a room sophisticated enough for the parents, yet one in which the children can feel at ease.

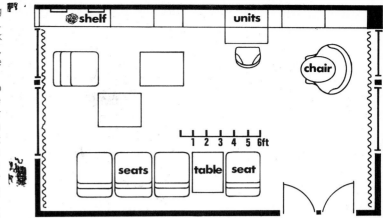

Room caters for both individual and group activities

LINK OLD AND NEW

The hauteur of the period proportions is softened by a subtle colour scheme. A deft combination of old and new helps to make the room welcoming

Arriving at a colour scheme is one of the most important aspects of planning a living room. The colours must be right for the proportions and period of the room, for the amount of light it gets, the kind of furniture and its scale. And, of course, the scheme must take into account existing pieces of furniture which cannot be changed and the owners' personal tastes.

In the gracious and relaxing living room shown here, the subtle colour scheme of warm shades of pale coffee, coral and brown, with plenty of white, may well have been inspired by the lovely faded shades of the two rugs — the oval Aubusson and the larger rectangular Bessarabian rug over which it is placed. Note that the patterns, far from clashing, seem to complement each other; the gentle floral Aubusson is set off by the clearer geometric pattern of the larger rug.

The pale coffee walls are a good foil for white paintwork and the simply framed modern painting set between the two French windows. These windows, beautifully proportioned, are a feature of the room. White bamboo blinds offer privacy when needed, while, when up, they allow in maximum light and a view of the trees outside. The white curtains are lined with coral. Off-white is used to cover the two simple settees, each with an open end, which form an L-shaped conversation piece. A square coffee table between them holds a table lamp and ornaments.

This is a seating arrangement that some people would quarrel with, as one settee is set partly in front of the window on the right. But it does not really obscure the view or the light and it is balanced visually by the coffee table placed at its end.

In line with the other settee, in the foreground, is a modern glass table on a steel frame. It is a perfect choice, as it does not hide any of the pattern of the beautiful rug on which it is placed. Its simple lines are at home in any setting.

A white ceiling shows off the decorative cornice and parquet floor in a room that is gracious without being forbidding, despite its haughty proportions.

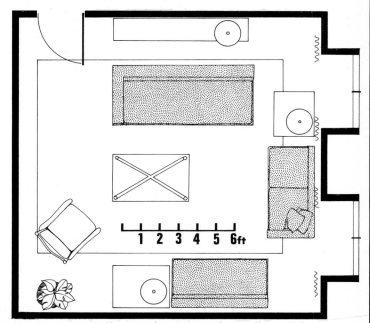

Three settees offer maximum seating using minimum floor space

BOLD IDEAS FOR AN

Panache has been applied in the decoration and furnishing of this living room — but without sacrificing the mellowness of a lovely old farmhouse

The furniture and furnishings in this delightful living room in a converted farmhouse have been chosen and applied with panache and unerring taste. The boldly modern and the appropriately traditional complement each other.

An unusual feature of this room is the treatment of the walls. They have been painted with nutmeg brown emulsion, while the beams and struts have been painted white. This is a reversal of the usual procedure in beamed houses, where the walls are normally white and the beams are either stained black or left their natural colour.

The furniture shows that like and unlike can harmonise. The capacious circular coffee table is painted white and nutmeg like the walls. Under the window a useful working corner is provided by the handsome black table on scarlet trestles, which match the scarlet Italian chair with its rustic rush seat.

No curtains obscure the view of the garden. A blind, which picks up the scarlet of the chair and trestles, makes a decorative feature when rolled down at night. There are bright touches of colour in the orange cushions by the fireplace and in the bright yellow pouffe, while a low ceiling light over the coffee table has a green glass shade.

There are, as there should be, country textures in the room: in the woven log basket, the rough weave of the cord carpet, the whitewashed brick of the fireplace and the mellow colours of the old embroidered picture over the mantelpiece. They all help to proclaim that this is a much loved country home.

Background heating throughout the house is provided by storage heaters. The glowing open fire provides the visible warmth which is such a comfort on cold evenings in the country.

Heating poses a problem for people using a country cottage as a week-end retreat. What is normally required is a quick temperature boost from zero or near zero. Storage heaters are the preference of many week-enders.

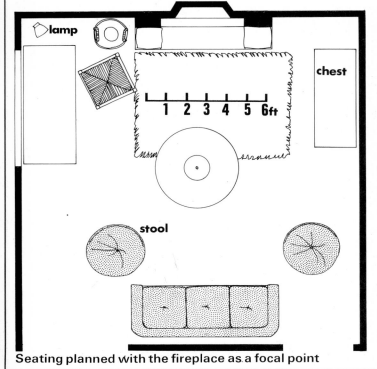

Seating planned with the fireplace as a focal point

STUDY WELCOMES

FAMILY INVASION 20

There's something of the 'den' about this charming room away from the main living area of the house and comfortably furnished for paper work or relaxation

The living room in a family home has to be all things to all members of the family. So if there is space to use another room as a 'bolt hole' for Father to retreat from the beat of the latest pop record, or for teenage children to use for homework or to entertain their own friends, it can make a substantial contribution to family harmony. If there is adequate space on the site of the house, a second auxiliary sitting room can sometimes be added on. The charming room pictured here did in fact start life as the conservatory extension to an early Victorian house.

When the present owners moved in, they found that some of the windows had been boarded up. They left them as they found them and cleverly compounded the disguise, covering them and all the walls with a soft blue rayon/silk fabric. The remaining windows that actually serve as such have blinds in the same fabric, giving a uniform effect at night and, during the day, plenty of light where it is wanted, over the desk.

Space in this room has been ably deployed. Bookshelves are built in on two walls to the same height as the windows. A shelf at window sill level runs all the way round the room and accommodates a lamp and ornaments. Near the desk there is plenty of room for papers in the small chest with abundant drawer space, and magazines and papers are neatly piled on a lower chest on the other side of the desk.

The seating in the room is provided by a deep Victorian chesterfield and a pretty spoon-backed Victorian armchair, both covered in soft green, which looks very effective against the blue walls. The pedestal chair has been painted green to match the upholstery and, on the wall, the softly coloured pictures of early balloons complete the decorative theme.

These days few people have a conservatory which they can convert. Those fortunate enough to have a workroom or study normally find it too small to double as an auxiliary sitting room. But ready-made room extensions are available from manufacturers in a large variety of sizes and finishes. Such an extension could be furnished to make a charming modern version of a study cum sitting room.

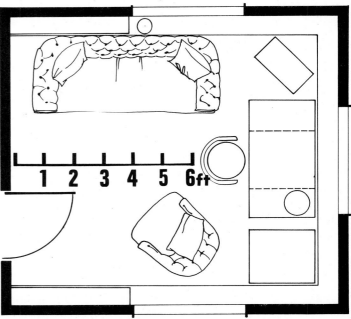

Plan of the room that was once a conservatory

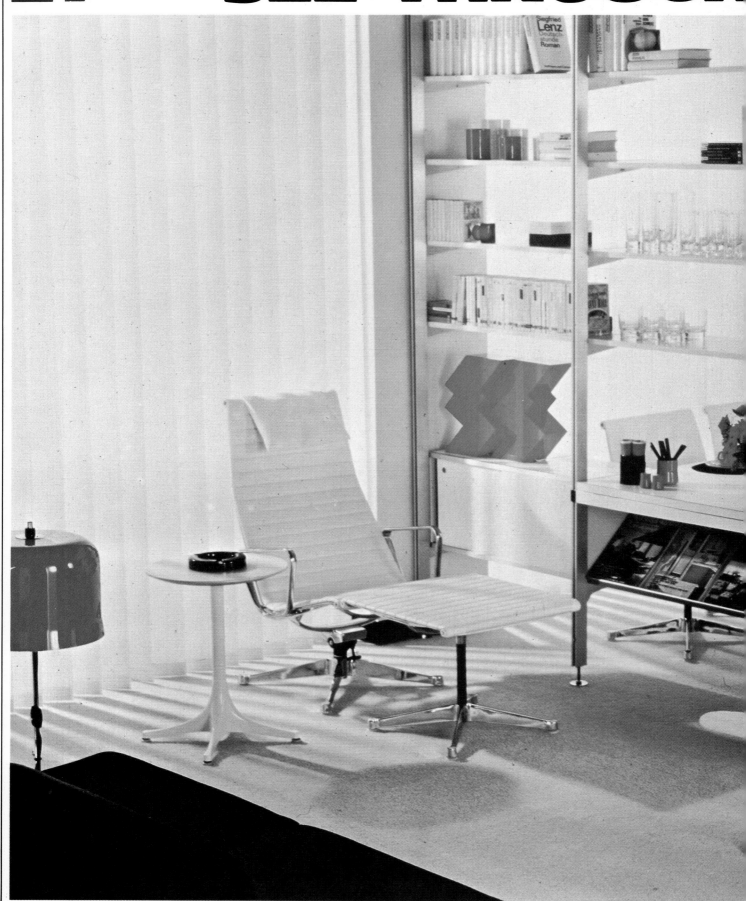

DIVIDES, BRIDGES

It divides a small area without constricting it. It is decorative and airy. It displays and it stores. And the dining table is attached

Dividing a room as small as this into two presents a major problem. It could result in making one small room look like two minute ones.

In the living room shown here the problem has been overcome through the use of a delicate, light-filtering divider unit.

Suspended on an aluminium framework, which goes from floor to ceiling, are cupboards with sliding doors and a neatly angled shelf for magazines on the living room side in the foreground of the picture. The dining side has a table, big enough to seat four comfortably, that actually hinges on to the unit. The tops of the cupboards act as mini sideboards.

Five rows of shelves hold glasses and books and a striking piece of modern sculpture, bright red — like many of the other ornaments in the room. The shelves are sparsely filled, deliberately, in order not to lose the graceful appearance of the unit and the sense of space which comes from being able to see through it.

The way colour is used in this small living room adds to the feeling of lightness. All the furniture is white, with the exception of the deep blue settee. The carpet is off-white. Red is used in disciplined touches: the sculpture, the shade of a table lamp, a coffee set and a large ashtray.

In keeping with the size of the room, cumbersome furniture has been eschewed. The handsome armchairs have metal frames and pedestal bases. The coffee tables have small tops on long-stemmed elegant bases. Everything is designed to take the minimum of floor space without sacrificing comfort.

If you are going to install a room divider, invest in the best fitment you can afford. An ugly one will stick out like a sore thumb, for it is not going to be a minor piece of furniture hidden in a corner but the main feature in the room. Care is needed in the choice of things displayed on a see-through divider. They will be on view from both sides, so make sure they are not too large or overpowering. A see-through unit is a good place to display a collection of coloured glass. Shining through, the light makes the most of the colours.

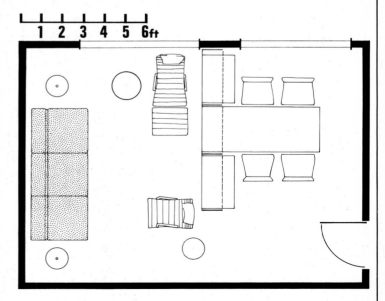

Note how divider with table attached saves floor space

FURNISHED TO LOOK

With its grass green carpet and fuchsia pink furnishings and floral paper, this enchanting small living room has the freshness of a garden in full bloom

From the graceful antique furniture to the colours sparked off by the pots of flowering plants in the jardinière near the window, everything in this room is pretty and fresh as a summer garden.

Just as a manicured green lawn sets off a garden to advantage, here the grass green rug in the centre of the room (which seems almost to have a grass texture about it) is a marvellous foil to the rest of the colours used. Fuchsia pink velvet makes the cushions for the two white-painted armchairs, and the same velvet is used for a floor-length cloth to cover a small round table.

The wallpaper is strikingly modern in this period setting and yet fits in beautifully. It is a stylised design of large green poppies and pink apple blossom, and it is used on facing walls, with the other two walls painted white. An unusual note: the skirting has been painted bright green to pick up the colour of the rug.

Soft gold, the colour of primroses, is the other colour gracing this room. It is used in the upholstery of the day bed and in the shade and base of the graceful table lamp.

Some of the furniture in the room is in a subtle grey-green, including a decorative clock and a wardrobe with glass doors covered with fabric. A period mirror near the window and sheer white curtains, with a strong pink border inset, complete the furnishings.

The colour scheme is the most interesting thing in this room. The owners have succeeded in doing what nature does all the time so successfully – mix strong colours with a sure hand. Bright green and fuchsia is all right in the garden, but indoors . . . ? Well, it works provided that everything else is right – in this case the very pretty and delicate furniture, the small quota of strong pink and the use of fresh white.

The right shade of clear green is a good mixer with other clear colours indoors just as it is in nature. Try mixing green with clear yellow and a lot of white; or with bright blue, again with a lot of white, and you will achieve a fresh and endearing colour scheme.

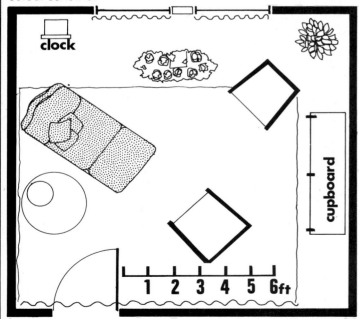

Minimum of furniture, informally arranged, suits small room like this

Instead of a conventional arch, an enchanting large 'porthole' gives access to the dining room. Another original note: a mirror wall of silver plastic

The owners of this unusual room meant to knock down the wall between the small living room and the dining room next door, but the wife, who is an artist, suggested just cutting a large hole in the centre of the wall instead. This meant inserting a steel girder as support, because the wall was load-bearing. But the effect is enormously striking, particularly as the curve of the circle is echoed in the circular or semi-circular lines of the very inexpensive furniture, which is, in fact, made of paper, and in the globe of the large lantern.

Another original idea in this room is the use of silvered plastic that simulates mirror glass. It is stretched along the whole of the wall on the left and makes the room look bigger. The material is stuck on with strong impact adhesive. It is much cheaper than using actual glass to achieve a mirror wall.

The cheerful colour scheme is white and orange with just one dark brown chair for contrast. Bright scatter cushions add colour and comfort. The dining room through the 'port-hole' — mind the step! — is decorated in the same colours, with white walls, white rugs, orange curtains and white blinds. The dining room has a low ceiling light over the table.

It is interesting to see how one bold and truly original touch — in this case, cutting a circle in the dividing wall — has given an inexpensively furnished room a truly exclusive air. But even the more common treatment of cutting an arch in the wall between a living and a dining room can work wonders and make each room appear larger. Always check with a builder, however, whether the wall is load-bearing or not. If it is, you can still cut your arch, but you must insert extra support.

The advantage of inserting an opening in the communicating wall, without bringing it right down, is that each room retains a measure of privacy and you still have the retaining wall on which to hang pictures or to use for storage units.

And if you cannot afford a whole mirror wall and do not fancy silver plastic, quite small wall-mounted or self-standing mirrors give an illusion of space if they are used in the right places.

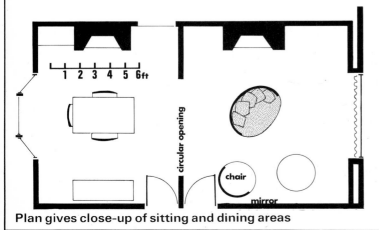

Plan gives close-up of sitting and dining areas

THE DINING ROOM

Two rounded settees embrace the intimate sitting circle in the middle of a white, airy room that is eloquently stylish

The 'island' seating unit in the centre and the virtually all-white decor endow this outstandingly original room with light and spaciousness.

The walls are white, the floor is in white vinyl tiles and the furniture is white, with brown, in the covers of the cushions and seats, as the only accent colour.

Grouping the seating in a circle in the centre leaves the rest of the room free for storage, and for dining or working at the trestle table under the window. It also makes for a cosily enclosed feeling in the conversation area. The semi-circular settees are grouped round a novel circular coffee table. Glass-topped, it has a hole in the middle in which a highly tolerant plant appears to be growing quite happily — there is no accounting for tastes in the plant world and you will find plants to suit most situations in your home! A brown fur rug beneath the coffee table gives warmth and softness underfoot and a clutch of patchwork cushions provides the only pattern. There is a wall-mounted electric fire.

Along one wall a series of fitments includes cupboards, houses a storage heater and the television set. All the corners of the fitments are rounded, perhaps to echo the circular theme in the centre of the room. They are topped by three rows of glass shelves on metal supports which hold books and ornaments.

For dining or working, the simplest of trestle tables is placed under the window and plain off-white blinds instead of curtains offer privacy. Shallow curved skylights above the windows are left unscreened.

Everything in this room is simple: a plain white glass wall light, unfussy modern ornaments. Yet the result is not coldness but eloquence.

One test of good interior design is its degree of versatility. This room more than passes muster. It could be made into a bed-sitter. The storage space frees the centre from clutter. There is space at one end for a divan bed. Animated guests in their magic world in the middle of the room would hardly realise they were in a bed-sitter.

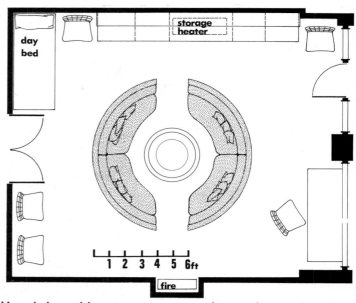

Here is how this room was arranged around central seating

Behind the cupboard doors are rooms-within-a-room and a wall ladder leads to the gallery bedroom in this space-saving highly decorative living area

This comfortable living room *plus* is full of surprises.

The cupboard doors hide a bathroom and a small fitted kitchen. When closed, the doors form an attractive feature, with their white paint, nice moulding and brass handles.

A wooden ladder leads up to the gallery and bedroom in the space above the bathroom and kitchen. It is just large enough to accommodate a bed, with pine shelves as a bedhead and a pine chest providing storage at the foot of the bed. There is a pretty chair, a patchwork quilt is used as a bed cover and an interesting mixture of pictures hang in groups all along the bedroom wall.

The actual living area is welcoming. The warm colour of pine is everywhere — from the old floorboards, which have been sanded and sealed, to the furniture, which includes a large and ornate cupboard with a full length mirror and drawers, and an attractive striped desk. Black and white fur rugs give a touch of luxury, and a deep, high-backed chesterfield in green striped velvet provides comfortable seating.

The white walls with their attractive moulding make a perfect background for the multifarious pictures which are one of the features of the room. They hang everywhere, in groups dictated by their size, the shape of the frames and the proportions of the wall space.

Together with a gilt mirror, pictures make the most of the small fireplace. Library steps are used to hold a table lamp and to display ornaments. A paper lantern hangs high on the lofty ceiling and a sturdy coffee table stands in front of the large French windows, which lead on to the room's treasured bonus — a pretty balcony overlooking a garden square.

Every inch of space has been put to good use, and every piece of furniture, picture and ornament chosen lovingly to create a charming atmosphere. There are lessons here for anyone living in a small flat.

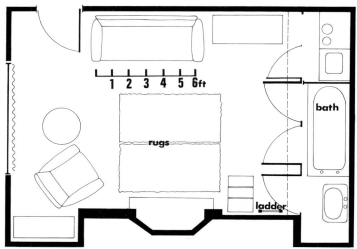

Bathroom and kitchen use under a quarter of total floor space available

LIFE STYLE ·SEE HERE

The living room is the family 'front'

There was a time, and within living memory, when even modest small houses in town or suburbs boasted a whole hierarchy of 'living' rooms, just as their quite modest owners boasted a whole hierarchy of paid skivvies ranking from the cook, mistress in the kitchen, to the junior maid at the beck and call of everybody.

The compartmentalisation of the house probably reached its apotheosis in Victorian England. In a not particularly sumptuous house there might be a morning room, a drawing room (reserved for Sunday afternoons, guests and momentous family occasions), a sitting room and a dining room — not to mention the bedrooms, the nursery and servants' quarters in basement or attic. Up and down the social scale the nomenclature varied. A withdrawing room (up) was in effect a drawing room. So was a front room (down). A parlour or snug (down) was the sitting/dining room.

The idea that all these small compartments, some hardly used from one festive season to another, should be combined into a single multi-purpose area for domestic living would have struck our forebears as flippant if not bordering on impropriety.

For one thing, in a bourgeois household the diktat was that children should be seen and not heard — and preferably not seen either. The nursery was the place for them, except at bedtime when they would be ushered into the parental presence in the sitting room or drawing room. Intolerable would have been the notion, had it been held, that children might view television, munching away, while their parents discussed their overdraft within earshot in the same room.

For another thing, our forebears believed in keeping up an impenetrable front before guests. There must be no hint in the form of a slightly frayed rug or a chipped table that domestic finances were at a low ebb. There must be no indication in the form of rumpled cushions, withering house plants or tarnished silver that housewifely duties (for whatever good reason) were being neglected.

The family could only keep up a decent front to outsiders if there was a room reserved for the purpose.

Today, we are all supposed to be much more free and easy, inside as well as outside the home. Who cares if unexpected guests plump down on easy chairs that are on their last springs or that they have a direct view from the living room of unwashed dishes stacked high in the kitchen? The answer probably is that most people, though far less socially formal than their parents or grandparents were, are still houseproud and *do* care. The warren of small rooms has given way to one major living area in most houses, not because people are less houseproud but because of the need to use space to its maximum potential and minimise the chores of cleaning and maintenance, few households these days being fortunate enough to retain the services of an occasional charwoman, let alone living-in servants.

Indeed, the fact that the living room may have to serve a variety of purposes tends to make it a more, rather than less, sensitive area. Ninety per cent of the time it may be where members of the family, including the children, gossip, argue, read, watch television, play games together or separately and have their meals. But ten per cent of the time it may have to wear at least the semblance of a party suit to greet guests. It is a room threatened with a split personality, and the more uncompromising its open plan the greater the chance of the split showing. Anybody who in the early evening has had to clear up — in preparation for a hoped for elegant dinner party with soft lights and affluent undertones — a room that the children have clearly used as their rumpus area all day knows only too well the problem of reconciliation.

Which is why a living room has to be planned to reconcile a variety of functions, domestic and social, without placing too much of the burden on the energy, time and ingenuity of the householders. A scheme of decoration that, with benefit of drapes and versatile lighting, can switch in mood from easy going domesticity to welcoming hospitality; adequate and flexible seating that can be adapted to any occasion in a matter of minutes; plenty of storage space where the family's untidy or over-revealing trappings can be quickly stowed away; and plenty of display space to show off to advantage what the family *does* want to reveal to guests, be it prize porcelain or the gilt-edged invitation to a private viewing ... all these factors rate highly in the planning of a multi-purpose living room.

In a much quoted phrase, Le Corbusier, the architect, proclaimed that a house was a machine for living in. Well, perhaps architecturally. But making a house into a home is, and is likely to remain — a human, not a mechanical, exercise. Although you can buy an automatic washing machine for the kitchen and modular storage units for the living room, you cannot buy a package labelled 'Home'. The simple adage rings true. Home — like life — *is* what you make it, and it takes a lot of making. It expresses a life style whether you particularly care about a life style or not.

A little time ago a firm of furniture manufacturers were worried because their widely advertised range was not selling as well as they had hoped. They observed that trendy clothes for young women and beauty aids were things that were being successfully marketed right across the board — after allowing for the different cost levels of furniture on the one hand and clothes and beauty aids on the other. Yet surely, said the furniture firm, personal appearance was far more individual than the appearance of a home.

Some elaborate market research ensued. And the furniture manufacturers concerned, who now hedge their bets on a wide range for varying tastes rather than majoring on a single range, concluded that you can tell more about people from their living room than from the way they dress.

A GLOSSARY ON LIVING ROOMS

Here is a guide to the basic components that make up a comfortable and serviceable living room

Flooring

To skimp on flooring is a false economy. This is the part of the living room that takes the hardest beating, so it is worth spending money here, even if it means that you have to wait longer to buy other furnishings. What qualities does living room flooring need? Durability; attractive appearance; noise-deadening effect; resistance to the kind of things that may be spilt on it, such as drinks and cigarette ash, and easy maintenance.

The types of flooring that measure up best to these requirements are as follows:

Carpeting. This is warm underfoot. If fitted wall to wall, it can be cleaned just by running a vacuum-cleaner over it, and shampooed in the

Dirt and stains show up less on patterned carpets

Hair cord makes a tough and durable floor covering

general Spring clean. Go for a good quality that wears well, such as an 80 per cent wool and 20 per cent nylon mix. Otherwise, try a hardwearing and less expensive cord, such as sisal. Areas of the room that are particularly vulnerable to wear and tear are in front of the fireplace (if there is one) and sofa. Protect these areas by putting down rugs. If your budget is really stringent, you can economise by using good quality carpet only in the centre of the room, and running felt over the outer edges.

Hardwood block flooring wears well and looks attractive. Interlocking panels come in kit form for do-it-yourself laying. This type of floor can be combined with a carpet in the centre.

Vinyl-coated cork. The insulating and sound-proofing qualities of cork complement the protective, easy-clean qualities of vinyl to give the best of both materials. Vinyl-coated cork is a particularly suitable surface for a family room where small children are liable to drop food on the floor. Rugs will add a warm touch in winter.

If you have inherited a wooden board floor, this can be sanded and then sealed with several coats of transparent sealer. Here again, rugs will add warmth to the floor.

Heating

On chilly evenings you may well find that, however efficient your central heating system, auxiliary spot heaters are needed to boost the 'local' temperature, especially if the living room is capacious and open-plan. Two spot heaters held in reserve may meet the need. There is little doubt that a room, however adequate the air temperature may be through central heating, can *seem* cold for lack of a visible heat source — an open fire or a gas or electric heater. A focal heat point is an important asset when you are entertaining guests. A manually controlled fan heater blows out hot air at a choice of speeds and warms up a whole room very quickly.

There is little point in heating up a room only to find that the hot air is escaping through ill-fitting doors and windows. Good insulation in the form of stick foam-backed tape can be applied by home handymen and is inexpensive. Double glazing halves the amount of heat lost *through the glass* in the room. Its contribution is proportionately greater if your windows are large.

If you have radiators in the living room, the most logical place for these is under a window — to act as a barrier against cold air entering the room. Many people think that to put full-length curtains over the radiator will cause heat loss,

A focal heat point gives visitors a warm welcome

but this is not the case. Within ten minutes, the curtains will soak up the heat from the radiator and direct it back into the room. Thick, interlined curtains are excellent draught-proofers and 'radiators' in themselves.

Lighting
A centre light tends to draw the eye from perhaps more attractive points of the living room and to cast light in only one area, leaving the outer edges in semi-darkness. Aim for pools of light set around the sides, with spot lighting at the vantage points for reading, sewing or study.

The darker the decoration scheme of the living room, the brighter your lights will need to be. On the other hand, a white ceiling and walls will bounce light back into the room.

Choose different types of bulb to fit the purpose you require — clear glass only for close work

Spot lighting is essential for close work

or to illuminate very dark corners; opaque or tinted bulbs for the areas of the room that need softer lighting.

A dimmer switch can be fitted in place of an existing switch. This gives you a means of adjusting the level of the light in the room. There are also switches to control the brilliance of table and standard lamps; and dual-control switches for controlling light levels in two separate lamps from the same socket.

The best lights to work by are those fitted on an adjustable stem, with a shade that concentrates the beam.

If the living room encompasses the dining area, the latter is one place in the house where a centre light is advisable. It should be set low over the middle of the table.

When you are planning the position of the furniture in your living room, bear in mind where you are going to want light plugs — or where they are already situated — and avoid putting heavy furniture in front.

Walls and ceilings
The most common types of covering for walls are paint, paper and fabric; and, for the ceiling, paint and paper. These can be coverings that can be used to highlight a particular area of the room, or to give the whole room an original flavour. Examples include wood panelling, decorative laminates and colourful tiles.

What you in fact use must be a matter of personal taste, governed, too, by the nature of the room and, not least, by consideration of who is going to undertake the decorating — professionals or yourselves. Paper or fabric, for example, give a more luxurious finish than paint but paint is probably simpler for an amateur handyman to apply.

If you choose paint, you are probably aiming

or a fairly practical type of living room. Settle for a washable paint, and keep a spare tin for touching up chips at a later date. Emulsion can be applied straight over an old paper which is in good condition. Badly cracked surfaces should be lined with a thin paper before putting on the paint. The easiest paint for a home handyman to use is one of the thick, non-drip varieties, and it is often possible to achieve a satisfactory result with only one coat.

If you choose wallpaper or fabric, you will get a textured finish that can look most attractive. Papers come in all sorts of patterns and surfaces. Vinyl-coated is particularly practical for a family room, since it can be wiped clean; it is generally available in a ready-pasted form which just has to be cut to lengths and soaked in water to hang. More delicate papers need careful handling and are better left to the experts. Bold patterns may give the amateur a headache when it comes to matching up the joints. Papers made with a matching curtain fabric are fun to look at and can brighten up an otherwise dull room.

Fabric on the walls is becoming increasingly popular. In many cases, it is no harder to apply than wallpaper, but here again delicate varieties should be left to the experts.

Furniture

Genuine antiques, antique reproduction or modern furniture? Antiques, if you can afford them, rate as treasured possessions and are an excellent investment. There is no reason why antique furniture cannot be put into a simple modern setting and blended with modern pieces.

But the principle to follow is that patently genuine materials mix best with patently false;

Folding cushions are a cheap form of extra seating

for example, old oak mixes better with laminated plastic than a bad reproduction of itself.

For people who cannot afford the time to search for antiques or the money to buy them but who still want the traditional look, the answer is to buy reproduction furniture. While much so-called reproduction furniture is junk,

Two sofas occupy less space than several armchairs

authentic copies of genuine antiques are made with the solid good-looks and craftsmanship in which our forbears specialised. The choice of woods is mainly between dark oak, mahogany, light pine and yew. If you want the furniture to look at least a century old, go for the special 'distressed' finish that it is possible to buy.

Modern trends in furnishing have led to some spectacular innovations, particularly in seating. Pedestals (instead of four legs) which permit the chair to tip and swivel; synthetic resins that cover a wood surface to save it from wood worm; a cup shape of injected mould plastic filled with foam to make a more durable and comfortable chair than a wood frame and horse-hair cushion ever did.

Then there are the sectionals — or seating units that can be used individually or put together to form a settee. Some of these even include a coffee table in the design. And they can be bought separately as domestic finances permit. However, if you buy units in stages, guard against choosing light colours, which will be shown up by the addition of a new unit. There are special pieces designed to fit into awkward corners and ranges to go around the walls — an idea that would not have been very practical in the days before central heating!

Storage

Most families are compulsive magpies, and storage needs in the living room must be

Open shelves are the cheapest form of storage

assessed with an eye on the future as well as the present. Items to be stored fall into two basic categories: those that the family wants permanently displayed; and everyday equipment that must be easily accessible but is better kept unobtrusive or even out of sight when not in use.

The first category generally consists of a number of small articles such as glass ornaments, ivory elephants, china or whatever. These can, of course, be displayed on an open shelf or mantelpiece, but here they are subject to dust and possibly damage. The best way to display them, yet at the same time protect them, is in a glass-fronted cupboard.

The second category probably comprises the bulk of possessions to be found in the living-room, ranging from the television set and hi-fi equipment (which can be arranged to make a visually attractive feature of the room, whether in use or not) to fireside games and albums (best kept invisible when not in demand).

Shelving is the simplest and probably the cheapest means of storage. But consider care-

fully the load the shelves will have to carry before making your choice of system; some are more secure than others. And, if you are building your own shelves, use inset supports which are usually stronger than end supports.

Wall storage units are more ingenious than shelves. Today's designers have produced a considerable range of highly versatile units that come singly, in a variety of sizes, and can be put together to add up to almost any combination. These offer the advantage that you can add to them at will and alter their sequence as you like. They can also be taken with you if you move, whereas built-in storage has to stay with the house.

If you have a large living room which doubles as a dining room, a partial 'wall' of free-standing storage units will effectively divide the room and house the cutlery, television set, books and so on at the same time.

A coffee table with a shelf or a built-in box below makes useful extra storage. So, too, does the traditional chest. But don't use the lid for displaying heavy ornaments that have to be moved each time the chest is opened. Use it instead, as extra seating accommodation.

Full-length curtains add height to a low room

Built-in storage units house possessions neatly